"Wow . . . just wow! Darcie Elizabeth's life-changing book is a transformative guide on how to release the energetic ties that are holding us back around our life and money. Once gone, more fun, more possibility and of course more money flows in!"

-Casey Tramp, MD Functional Medicine and Family Medicine Practitioner Owner, Sastun Direct www.sastundirect.com

"*More Money, More Power?* is a practical book, non-fluff and hardcore full of wisdom. These teachings will help you release the power money has over you and your life."

-Susanne Grant, Business Coach & Consultant - Success without Sacrifice, Grant Method - Business Coaching & More www.grantmethod.com

"In *More Money, More Power?*, Darcie Elizabeth exposes the energetic component of financial flow and presents a fresh new perspective of our personal relationships with money. This impactful book gives us tools to detect and tear down the deeply ingrained patterns that prevent us from allowing money into our lives."

-Dr. Jessica Tallman, D.C. Doctor of Chiropractic and Owner of Mind and Body Family Wellness Inc., Lenexa, KS www.mindandbodykc.com

"In *More Money, More Power?* Darcie takes the guess-work out of our relationship to money and makes it seem not only possible but so much easier to reach our goals than we've realized. If you are looking to have your mind blown, rapid personal growth and your bank accounts expanded, this is your road map!"

-Mallory McClelland, Psychic Business Coach www.mallorymcclelland.com

"Darcie's *More Money, More Power?* spoke right to my soul and will be one of the most important books of our time! As we search for that elusive power hiding behind those dollar signs, Darcie's clear and powerful guidance shows us that the power is in us all along, and how to clear away the debris, so we can finally shine with ease. A must-read for everyone claiming their true wealth!"

-Lola T. Small, Best Selling Author, Educator, Activist www.lolasmall.com

MORE MONEY MORE POWER MORE MONEY MORE POWER MORE MONEY MORE POWER?

UNCOVER YOUR UNIQUE MONEY DESIGN TO DISCOVER
THE KEY TO YOUR INNATE POWER AND WEALTH

DARCIE ELIZABETH

Published in Canada for Global Distribution by Golden Brick Road Publishing House Inc. Printed in North America.

ISBN: paperback: 9781989819036, ebook: 9781989819043

Author: hello@darcieelizabeth.com

Media: hello@gbrph.ca

Book orders: orders@gbrph.ca

CONTENTS

SECTION 3: RECLAIM

PREFACE

Hi reader, I'm Darcie and I'm so grateful that we are crossing paths. Before you dive into *More Money, More Power?: Uncover Your Unique Money Design to Discover the Key to Your Innate Power and Wealth* and the accompanying e-course, I wanted to share why I created this resource and how this work has drastically impacted my life.

But first, let's talk about the question I get often from those who are new to my work as a former CPA turned Energetic Money Consultant. The question of why I decided to bridge what looks like seemingly two different worlds: practical money applications, and a spiritual and energetic approach to manifesting your goals and desires. I walk this path not because I was born gifted with the knowledge and application to weave these two seemingly different aspects together, but because I had to muddle my way through this work to support myself, first.

I'm the first to admit that when it came to my personal financial experience that it hadn't always been rosy. High consumer debt coupled with a pattern of living paycheck to paycheck created an environment where I continually pushed off my dreams while I waited for money to show up. Money to pay off our debt, to create a solid savings plan, to feel more comfortable as a way of permission before I took action towards what I truly wanted: to write books and travel the world with my family.

In my late twenties, my husband and I were starting a family and found ourselves facing the fact that we had an unhealthy relationship with money. Distinct patterns were coming into our awareness, that no matter how hard we tried, we could not seem to dig our way out of. As a CPA, having practical knowledge and tools that should have been able to help us paint a different financial reality, I grappled with the emotional aspects of why I could help others through my day job but couldn't seem to get ahead financially for myself. At the same time, holistic and alternative techniques began to float into my awareness. I was introduced to the term *money mindset* and the concept of our energetic body—opening my awareness to a deeper level that I wasn't aware existed. I began to see a reality where there was much more than met the eye and found ways to access this unseen, intangible information through connecting more deeply with my body and through God/Spirit. This journey led me to discovering tools to help balance my body on an unseen and energetic level while going through my spiritual awakening, finding myself on the other side in an entirely new and strengthened relationship with God.

Once I dove in, I was a runaway freight train that couldn't have been stopped even if I tried. I began to uncover and implement various techniques and teachings from teachers and mentors to apply to my relationship with money through the patterns I saw before me. Why did we seem to rack up debt just as quickly as we paid off a balance? Why, no matter how much we tracked, brought in, and saved did we seem to have "just enough" at the end of each month? And why did this create such anxiety and panic within me? What parts of me on a subconscious level were actually comfortable in these patterns and didn't feel worthy to receive more than what I was seeing before me now? My curiosity and willingness to explore took me through profound experiences that led me here: on a never-ending journey where I've been able to explore how I can dive even deeper into my own work (because I fully believe this growth process will never end), embody that transformation, and share the process (and shortcuts) with you.

My relationship to money went from an incredibly disempowered state to engaging with it as a neutral tool. In the past money seemingly had all the power over me: my emotional state, how I moved through my life, and the choices I made were determined by this number (or lack thereof). As I began to cultivate tools to dive deeper into why this was my experience with money, I discovered how to enter into neutrality with money as a tool and move through life in an empowered state. The roles didn't reverse and I didn't feel as if I held power over money, money simply was no longer an obsessive thought in my mind. It was a tool to support me. As I moved out of the unhealthy attachments to it, it lost its power and no longer seemed to create the drama in my life it once had. This, for me, was the foundation for a healthy relationship with money. And if you have dreams and goals that you've felt unable to move towards, the foundation of your relationship to money likely holds the key to shifting that perception.

After taking myself through the foundational work around healing my relationship to money I was able to create financial freedom through my business, which quickly led to creating time and location freedom. Something I'd longed for since we started a family seven years ago. It also enabled us to take big, bold action. When you move into a more neutral relationship to money and drop the drama around it, it's suddenly easier to take big, bold action. It's a given that you should now go after your dreams, pivot and experience life the way you truly desire to. Without consciously and intentionally going through this work, my creative expression when it came to living life on my terms was stifled. This pivotal work with money enabled us to create the time and location freedom to plan a year-long worldwide travel adventure with our kids. Unfortunately, we chose the year 2020 so it ended up looking much different than we had planned. But the best part? Already going through the foundational work of healing our relationship to money, looking at where we derive our sense of safety and security from (within, not without) allowed us to move through 2020 with ease. Our flight to Ecuador was cancelled as the countries closed their borders less than twenty-four hours before we were set to leave. After selling seventy-five percent of what we owned and moving the rest to storage, our family of five was living out of six suitcases not entirely sure where we would rest our heads long-term. As fear set in across the world we were able to pull from the work that we've done to make decisions in the best interest for our family. Our year of travelling ended up being a year of adventures around America and we came to terms with that, quickly knowing that no matter where we were and what was going on in the world, we would be supported. At the peak of this fear and general sense of uncertainty, I received the urge to write this book. *What better time than now?* As we are collectively thrust into a world where the unknown and uncontrollable—which has always been there—is front and center, forcing us all to look at our discomforts around the reality that we've never really been in control at all.

This has given us all an incredible opportunity to look at where we each derive our sense of safety and security from; and in what ways we are entering into disempowered relationships with money and other forms of security—allowing us to take back the power we've given to these forms of security, take back the reins and charge ahead towards a life on your terms. This is the key to moving through the next decade (and beyond) with ease. And you can still choose to go after your dreams, take big, bold action towards your vision, and know that no matter what might be happening you will always be supported.

This small but mighty book packs a punch and is intended to be used in conjunction with the accompanying e-course. As you make your way through the book I recommend you create the time and space to go through the accompanying e-course in tandem. Take the awareness that the book will support you in opening up and then allow you to dive into the practical action that naturally comes next. The guided meditations, reflection questions, and more within the e-course will meet you exactly where you are now: whether that's step one or step one hundred when it comes to healing your relationship to money. You will be prompted throughout the book to access the e-course at various stages, or you can bookmark this page in your browser now ahead of time: www.more-moneymorepowerbook.com.

I'm so grateful you're here with me and send my love to you as you embark on this journey!

INTRODUCTION

Consider this book a love letter from me, to you. From the Universe, to your soul.

I invite you not only to read the words, but to feel them. Allow them into your heart. There's a lot of possibility wrapped up in these pages, or on your digital screen, and I want it to invite you into making the shifts you desire in your life. Think of this as a permission slip to allow your mind to let go of money, even just for a moment. Allow yourself to open up to the possibility that any money woes or problems you're experiencing might not really be about money under the surface—that your money issues could be holding up a smoke screen, keeping you from peeking into what's truly going on behind the fog. So let this book open you up to explore that money might not be all that it's cracked up to be; it might actually be a lot less powerful, a lot more mundane, and definitely a lot easier to grasp than many of us believe.

You will be guided in this book through the lens of your Money Design—a term I use that encompasses the reasons why you really do what you do with money. It's the below the surface, behind the cover reasons for why you act in ways that don't align with or get you closer to your financial goals and desires. It's that frustrating spending habit, climbing debt balance, or reluctance to charge what you desire to receive. Accessing your Money Design will help you dive into the why behind the why when it comes to your relationship to money. This will support you in looking past the very real action you are (or aren't) taking and into what precipitated it: the root. You will see how those actions stem from the pieces that are built within your Money Design: the subconscious beliefs and programming that are driving your current financial reality (we'll dive deeper in Chapter 3).

Looking at your life right now, you can start to explore these pieces by reflecting on the questions below. But first, let's bring awareness to your current financial situation: your income, business revenue, debt balances—the ins and outs of your financial world. Take a moment and sink into the reality of it as it stands at this moment. Now, reflect using the following questions:

What (in your opinion) needs to happen to improve your current financial situation? And why haven't those things happened yet?

A lot of awareness can come out of these two questions, so take a moment and think about them. Jot them down and uncover what you believe right now is standing between you and where you want to be. I'm going to guess when you think about your answers, a lack of trying or effort doesn't come up. I'm going to boldly make the assumption that you're not lazy either. Most of us are attempting to shift on the outer level, to shift our practical habits, without going to the root of why we have that particular habit in the first place. Think of a plant. If you wanted to remove a diseased bush from your garden, would you simply cut the top off and expect the problem to be solved? No, of course not. You would dig up the dirt around it and shovel all the way into the Earth to pull up every last piece of the diseased root to ensure the safety and health of the other plants in your garden. The same concept should be applied when it comes to shifting your relationship and connection to money. No outer shift or attempted habit change is going to solve the deeply rooted reasons as to why you are acting in ways that go against your goals or dreams. You have to go deeper. And that's where the beauty of diving in through your Money Design comes into play. It is a blueprint to show you why you're doing what you're doing with money at the root level.

I approach my work and these teachings from a heavily spiritual and energetic lens. While I have immense "practical" knowledge around money after spending over a decade working as a CPA, that's often not what's needed when someone is ready to shift their financial reality. It's an inside game. The inner work, diving into the subconscious and into the unseen energetic realm is where you'll find the deepest shifts. Of course, we can't be oblivious to the fact that financial literacy is sorely lacking from our society. But the same can be said about our emotional awareness when it comes to our finances. Understanding and being able to peel back the layers to see what is truly driving our financial habits and decisions is needed for long-lasting change to occur.

As you continue along this journey, I ask you to remain open to the unknown. Open to the idea that there are things you can't see with your physical eyes but that are as real as the piece of furniture you're sitting on. And as a result of engaging with these unseen pieces and creating intentions to work with the energetic parts of our world, you can enact great change within your life. This is true not only within your immediate sphere, but the ripple effect can move outward to enact positive change in those around you— Your family, clients, customers, friends, neighbors, and more. The light you shine within becomes a beacon for others to follow suit, helping you heal your relationship with money while giving others the possibility to do the same for themselves. Because in the end, when one of us succeeds, we all succeed.

We are amidst a great awakening in our world and within our society. The pieces of our lives that we accepted as uncomfortable but normal are no longer acceptable to our souls. Our standards have been raised; our eyes have been opened. We are being asked for more because we came here for more. And as our world changes to accommodate this great awakening and vibrational shift, our social structures inevitably will shift as well. Money is one of those shifting structures. The work within this book and the accompanying audio course will not only support you in moving *with* this shift but will support the world as a collective in healing as well. To move into a reality where all of our systems as a society are built on the foundation of love for all, rather than built on fear, power, and control-based programs that were designed to create a false sense of authority for one group of people over another.

As we make this inevitable societal shift with money, it's vital that we are deprogramming and deconstructing these systems within ourselves as individuals. We ourselves are not changing, in fact we are simply taking off layers of programming and conditioning that are clouding our true brilliance and expression. We will shift to look at our bodies and our energy systems as microcosms of the whole—of the Earth and our collective humanity. Think of this as doing your part. Healing your relationship to money will make it easier for you to step into your shoes as the magnificent co-creator of your life. And as such, the amazing life that you create will no doubt benefit many others, helping to lift humanity as a whole. We can all be happy, abundant, and free when we release the scarcity mindset and competitive nature that we've been programmed to embody when it comes to money.

We will be going through the process of deconstructing and deprogramming the old systems that are keeping you tied to the false belief that:

1. Power is outside you, and
2. To access power, you need to accumulate more money.

To do this we need to peel back the layers of your Money Design to move into a new neutral relationship with money, one that is no longer a tool used to validate or measure your worthiness, as no outside source will ever be able to fill that void.

This book was created to be deeply healing, immensely activating, and my hope is that it will push you to bring in new awareness to help you radically shift your connection to money. As you go through the book you will be guided to stop and reflect. These pauses are purposeful, so that you can integrate and process the information from the previous chapters. Be sure to stop, integrate, and reflect with the strategically placed reflection prompts to support you in deepening the work. There will also be links to guided meditations and visualizations to support you in this process. I urge you to participate, but above all else, listen to your inner guidance system. Your intuition and your body know what's best and what's needed for you.

Lean on these words before you as a guide to dive into the work that extends well beyond these pages and out into the world. Using all the resources I have made available to you within the accompanying e-course, you will be supported as you deeply connect to yourself and create real, lasting shifts to better your relationship to money.

I am thrilled that you are here to participate and tap into the energy and teachings within this book. Allow the words before you now to activate a new awareness that will guide you to begin uncovering your Money Design, allowing you to shift your Design to further align with the experiences that you came to create in this life. Your unique Money Design will help you stack the deck in your favor, to give yourself the courage to reclaim your personal throne and access the power, wealth, and fulfillment that can only come from within through your connection with God/Spirit.

Ready to begin? Let's begin to access this new awareness through Chapter 1's activation. *You also have the option of listening to Chapter One's activation through audio here: www.moremoneymorepowerbook.com

FREE YOURSELF

Wild laughter.

Pure joy.

Unbridled ecstasy.

Feeling more alive in this moment than you've ever experienced.

The lights flicker and turn to beckon you forward.

Your body halts as you abruptly come upon a clearing.

Allowing your body to catch its breath.

The sound of your thumping heart in your ears.

Drowning out the surrounding noises.

Allowing your body's tempo to slow as you take in the scene before you.

You notice your wet feet shift against the moss under you.

In front of you are hundreds, no thousands, of bright flickering lights.

Moving in time together, it's difficult to grasp if they're one consciousness.

Your eyes widen.

Your pulse quickens again at the scene before you.

You see the lights moving quickly, back and forth in communication.

Preparation.

What are they preparing for, you ask?

"We've been waiting for you," they say.

And suddenly a dozen bright, beautiful lights surround you.

Beckoning you to step within the clearing.

To enter this healing space where God/Spirit is inviting you to become one with the Earth again.

You feel safe.

You feel supported.

You feel seen.

You feel grounded and held.

As you make your way into the clearing, you're led toward a rambling river.

The clear water gently flows over the smooth, round rocks.

Here, you place your feet within the stream.

Your feet are lovingly washed. Caressed by the water.

"Your feet are sacred portals," the voices tell you.

Anchoring you to the Earth.

Stabilizing you into your physicality.

Whether you have physical feet or not.

Energetically this space is where you anchor.

In your pursuit of physical pleasure.

Physical experiences.

"That's what you're here for," they tell you.

Because why else would your soul have come here, to be within this physical body?

To experience.

To live.

To love.

To create.

To grow, for yourself and humanity.

Come back to your body in the present now.

Wherever you are in the world.

Right now, as you read these words.

And see your own light glowing within your body.

A spark, starting to fill the space you inhabit.

Rising and growing.

And feel the grid of glowing lights that are placed all over the world begin to connect.

Because we're all connected.

Bring awareness now to the rise and fall of your chest as you sit here.

The blood coursing through your veins.

Attention to your heart pumping within your chest to make all this a living reality, experience.

Working with you, for you, since before you left your mother's womb.

It hasn't stopped.

Hasn't taken a break.

It beats for you, every second of every day that you grace this Earth.

Close your eyes now and feel the gratitude for your heart space grow and let it build within you.

Pause.

Now invite this appreciation to expand and fill every corner of your heart.

Overflowing from this space to move freely throughout your body.

To all your cells, organs, tissues, bones.

Enveloping your entire body with gratitude.

With love.

With appreciation for this beautiful vessel that you get to call home.

Now bring attention down to your feet where you are now.

The soles of your feet.

And as you do, feel yourself magically being transported back to the clearing in the woods.

The beautiful lights waiting patiently.

Your feet are drying quickly in the warm sun as you shift to stand on a cool rock.

You notice an interesting sensation on the soles of your feet.

An opening, a tingling.

Even though you can't see it, the portals of your feet are widening.

You can sense it.

You can feel it.

You know it.

As they do, you see a swirling, light energy sourced by Spirit making its way up from the Earth below.

You watch as it circles and twists into a root-like structure.

You feel your body being activated by this energy at the soles of your feet.

Feel the tingle, the rush as your body reacts to the presence of this grounded, supportive energy.

Bringing you into your body in a more pronounced way.

A deeper way.

Almost as if you've become a part of this beautiful forest.

A moving part in the ecosystem.

As you take a step, the swirling energy lifts and follows you.

Keeping you rooted, grounded, supported with each step you take.

You follow your body's lead and walk over to a soft patch of moss.

You lay down and begin to watch the clouds pass overhead.

Minutes. Hours.

They pass by as you move from perch to perch enjoying the gifts of the forest.

Sights of the clearing.

The company around you.

With nowhere to be.

Nothing to do.

Enjoying the now starlit sky, feeling the weight of the present moment.

Fully present in the now.

Recognizing the harmony of the Earth, of the ecosystem around you.

Reveling in the beauty.

The inner workings of God. The Universe.

With each thought.

Each acknowledgment.

Each emotion.

Affirming your presence here.

You are allowing your own powerful light to build within.

Inviting it to continue building, growing.

To fill your entire being.

Until it reaches a fever pitch.

Overflowing with no choice *but* to move outward.

Cascading out of you and beginning to fill the clearing, spilling out into the forest.

As it does, it encircles the surrounding communities.

Cities.

Countries.

The entire world.

Sit for a moment and feel the breadth of this light that started within you.

The spark that was created by allowing this supportive energy from the Earth within.

As you send this energy out, the Earth continues to support you below.

You are simply a conduit to the magic of this beautiful union.

These resources, this support is never-ending.

You are always supported.

Feel the Earth sharing its gratitude for you.

For being here, for embarking on this journey.

For opening your heart and activating the deconstruction process.

For choosing to be initiated into this sacred energy exchange.

For allowing God/Spirit and the Earth to support and facilitate you on your path.

You're grounded.

Open.

Ready.

Now let's shine a light on the distortions and programs that you are ready to burn.

To release, so that you can move into a new way of *being* with money.

A way that supports you completely in creating the life you desire.

While being supported in a way that serves your highest potential and growth.

Are you ready?

To access this activation and initiation via audio, type www.moremoneymorepowerbook.com in any web browser to access the accompanying e-course to the book, and click "Activation" to listen in.

CHAPTER 2:
MONEY ISN'T THE
GOAL. IT'S A TOOL

*"Money represents wealth in
the same way the menu
represents dinner."*
-Alan Watts

After reading this book, my hope is you take away this: wealth is an inside game. Wealth and money are two entirely different concepts, neither needs the other in order to be present in your life. And how can we begin to understand that distinction? By looking at our conditioning around what we believe to be true about money and power. The societal conditioning around money has made it hard for us to accept our innate power and God-given purposes in this life, inhibiting us from embodying our innate wealth. The programming that has been inherited by you when it comes to money, your unique Money Design, often distorts your sense of personal value. Instead of recognizing your innate value by existing on this planet, you are conditioned to value yourself based on external markers and what you can do for, or provide to, society or others. This distortion undercuts your ability to move forward in your highest purpose with confidence, which leaves you in a state of disempowerment. It also restricts your ability to attract the resources you need to see your big visions, your big dreams, through to completion in the way you desire.

Think of it this way: our big, beautiful lights come into our physical bodies and into the constraints that society has developed at the moment we enter. We're beautiful square pegs trying to fit into a round, constricting hole. Something's got to give, and it doesn't have to be us.

With this awareness, I invite you to stay open to continue exploring this topic and how you can begin deconstructing your relationship to money (by diving into and playing with your unique Money Design) in order to create a path forward for yourself that allows you to embody your purpose, increase your fulfillment, re-discover your innate power, and as a by-product of those three things, experience and create true wealth. This leads to arguably the most important piece: allowing you to recognize the innate value in simply being present in your physical body, here experiencing this life as a co-creator through God/Spirit.

This is why we started this journey in Chapter 1 with an activation, to center your body and bring you back to Earth; to remind you that you are spirit here in this physical body having a beautiful physical experience; to bring you back to the bigger picture, the reason for your existence, and to the awareness that we're here for so much more than what we've filled our days with. There is so much more waiting for you to explore when you look past (what can be) the monotonous schedule that is filling your day. Opening up to the reality of your bigger purpose will give you the courage to make shifts in your reality toward what you desire, which starts by making shifts in your internal (subconscious) world.

There is one thing I need to be clear on before we dive in: our souls can't fully create on this planet without our physical, earthly bodies. We can't experience and realize these manifestations without physical, earthly support. Being provided for comes in all kinds of sizes and shapes—money being one tool to that end. From the intricate planet and its inner workings that create the perfect balance to allow for our existence, to our ecosystem, to the air we breathe—all are parts of the puzzle. When we think of our bigger picture within this vast creation, they are all supporting us. If they weren't running in perfect order, life as we know it wouldn't exist. You wouldn't be here, reading this book. So, although money is important as you live in today's world, money in a sense is a blip in the vast construct of safety and support on a Universal level. All the resources and support that is needed for you to live and thrive on this Earth can come to you in a myriad of ways. The key to growth is to open your receiving channels and allow them in.

How do you allow these receiving channels to open more fully to receive support, in this case money? By reawakening and stepping into the power that lies within you. The goal is to be able to stand in a place where there's no question whether you'll be supported, or if you'll have what you need to continue moving toward your purpose. Because being supported is inevitable when you're standing in your true power. Not the power that we believe comes from harnessing more money, or any other external markers like fame, fortune, or notoriety. But true power. The power that can only come from knowing where your true sense of safety and security lies: from God, the Universe, and all that is. When you can step into knowing that you will have all that you need (at all times) because you recognize your own innate value, there are no ifs, ands, or buts about it. You receive what you need because you exist. Simply put, you are always supported.

We all come into this life with a construct that allows us to utilize and receive the money and support we need to live and breathe in our purpose. That's what our Money Design is, all the pieces and parts that tell us how we are comfortable (on a subconscious level) in receiving and engaging with money and support. Your Money Design is meant to deconstruct and rebuild as you grow; to allow you to let go of your current conditioning around money which enables the rebirth process to occur; to move into the future to embody your goals and dreams. Over the course of this book we'll continue to dive into and break apart the belief that more money equals more power, while allowing you to begin looking at the power you have to create a new relationship forward with money, from the inside out.

And with that being said, we're here to talk about money. Money is an integral piece of our existence on Earth. We can't hide from it, nor should we. It's here co-creating along with us. It's an amazing tool that we can use to our advantage. What's keeping most of us from taking full advantage of it are the pieces within our unique Money Design—the layers of conditioning and programming that are upheld in the body that go against the belief that we are the creators of our lives and are innately worthy of receiving the support we desire.

What you believe you are capable of receiving (whether consciously or not) dictates what you do in fact receive. When it comes to engaging with the subconscious aspect of your relationship to money (your Money Design), you are changing what you believe you are capable of receiving and experiencing on an internal level first. This creates a correlating shift in what you do, in fact, receive. Think of it as an internal barometer. Your current Money Design is comfortable receiving at a certain level, it's what it was designed to do. If what you desire is outside that comfort level and exceeds the barometer's current standing, you have to shift your Money Design (a.k.a. the perception in your body) to allow yourself to receive that which you desire, or you have to shift what you desire to fall within this benchmark.

When it comes to your Money Design, there's no right or wrong. You are perfect and whole right where you are now, and no amount of money will ever change that. Shifting your Money Design is all about creating and being able to move into new experiences for yourself. It truly is an inner game that some of us are more than ready to play in our lifetime, while others are simply not going to be interested in. And both scenarios are perfect and valid.

When we look at our Money Design, the comfort level in which we receive, societal conditioning plays a role (which we'll dive further into in future chapters). Our current societal structures and the way we've been taught to operate and engage with money have created a misinterpretation of its true nature. It is a tool for exchange. So, when we look at shifting your Money Design to allow you to more easily receive, we need to first bring your connection to money back to its true nature to allow the full breadth of support in. What do I mean? We need to learn the true, neutral purpose of money and what it's here to do and how it can support us.

Before we dive into your unique, energetic Money Design, let's bring money back to its true, neutral purpose: what money is, why it was created, and what purpose it serves.

What is money, truly? Money was created as a tool to help us more easily account for and enter into exchanges of value. Money can only account for the dollars and cents that you've accumulated—at any given point—in this exchange, which hardly makes it a valid marker for wealth, as it's only valuable in the right context. Money in and of itself isn't the sole marker of wealth as it's only valuable in today's modern world in this context. Money—paper or coins—are valuable in today's world as a means for exchange; but what value does it hold in let's say (as an extreme example) an apocalyptic scenario? Likely none at all. In that scenario, what we deem to be valuable would likely be food, shelter, ammunition and the things that we would have to trade for them. In this scenario wealth and value would be judged on the tools needed to survive and thrive: a contraption to filter water, seeds to plant, weapons. These items would likely carry much more weight and value. An unlikely example? Maybe. But it shows that money is illusory. It accounts for the value that you provided to someone else, either in service or goods, or what you've been able to accumulate through gifts or other means in an easy to manage way. It's a number to account for something, nothing more and nothing less.

Actually, it's a piece of paper and I'm going to ask you to stay open to looking at it through a new lens. We're not going to get into the mechanics of how it's produced, what signals the production, and how it's circulated. Nor are we going to dive into the economy, capitalism, or how our monetary supply and demand fits into our world and everyday lives. We're going to talk about money as a concept, as a construct of our world. And then, we're going to deconstruct this concept through the lens of *your* Money Design.

Money at its root is a value for exchange. It's a tool. Before the construct of money was created, there was a bartering system. In this bartering system, you traded your services or the things you did have, in exchange for someone else's services or items. You decided the value placed on your services or items and entered into an agreement with the other person as to what would be an equal and fair exchange. You have ten chickens; you need one cow. Both parties agree that the trade value is fair, and you exchange and receive your goods.

As society evolved into less rural living and began to cluster within cities, the need arose for a tool to represent the value given to these services or physical items. Bartering became difficult as there was no standard or set value for what was exchanged as goods. As families began moving within the city limits, they also became more dependent on others instead of surviving in a close-knit community or family unit. Anthropologists date the origin of this shift to our current exchange system of money, back to Mesopotamia around 2500 BC[1] when silver rings were used in an exchange. These rings were used to define the services or physical products in a tangible fashion that was easier to discern. It's said that as the ease of this value exchange system began to spread, other Middle Eastern countries began to implement similar systems and abandoned the barter system. As society moved into this easily identifiable and quantifiable system, it also opened doors and made it easier for governments to begin implementing taxes and levying fines. It also paved the way for the original accounting systems, as governments felt the need to record these transactions within a ledger, in clay seals. And it also brought forth the original banking system, which was further developed by the Babylonians, with a system of loans and credit using the standard unit of exchange that had developed.

This movement toward a more standardized system took the responsibility away from the people and

---

1   Richard Marrison, "Ancient Mesopotamia Economy", HistoryTen, May 7, 2020 https://www.historyten.com/mesopotamia/ancient-mesopotamia-economy/

placed it on the structures that were built to regulate these transactions: banks, accountants, and a more robust government that could levy taxes. This was the dawn of our current financial systems that are still used now, over five thousand years later.

The move from agrarian living to a society more focused within the city also led to a more specialized focus when it came to living and moving through life. Families no longer needed to be skilled in many areas, instead one could focus and specialize. This shift, as you can imagine, led to faster growth as individuals could focus, hone their skills, and amplify their talents. It also led to a greater reliance on each other. Now society moved away from independently run households or smaller villages, and into a way of life that relied on all parts of the greater machine to run smoothly. The collective society, all parts of the machine, were vital and necessary.

As this shift occurred, it created the foundational pieces on which society has built our connection to money. As we birthed the systems that housed what the economic structures would be built upon, they mirrored the shift that was occurring within. Namely, less autonomy and control over our personal exchanges and the value that each person could give to them, coupled with more regulation around these exchanges. These systems lessened the focus on our internal value and what we bring to the table (literally and figuratively), and added more emphasis on what externally we had to account for our value (money). This internal to external shift regarding value is what we are being asked to reverse when it comes to moving forward in co-creating a life of wealth and fulfillment.

Fast-forward to the sixteenth century, Europeans were using banks and private institutions to borrow money and receive banknotes so that they didn't have to carry around coins. This paper money was issued by these institutions and eventually, it was issued by the government like it is today. This shift to paper money helped to increase international trade and kicked off a new trend. Countries and upper-class individuals began to buy currencies from other countries to create a currency market. Essentially, the holdings of these currencies could be used as a form of bargaining when it came to what was coined the "currency wars." Countries that were at odds with each other could attempt to shift the value of the other country's currency by driving the value up and making their country's trade goods too expensive to buy. Or they could drive the value down, and therefore decrease the income generated by a country and affect their ability to fund a war or eliminate their ability to survive completely.

Money, which began as a way to quantify and create a standard in exchanges of goods between two people, picked up alternative uses over the years and magnified. This once neutral tool used for exchanges became a way to levy taxes and fines on the people, created a vacuum where this tool was necessary for purchasing, and was used as a tool for warfare against entire countries and their populations. Although a neutral tool at its inception, it has been wielded in arguably unhealthy ways in the span of its existence. As we speak today, this tool is continually shifting and as we shift as a collective, it will continue to shift along with us.

As mentioned earlier, we have immense power to shift our social structures. Our engagement, our attention, and our willingness to uphold them in an energetic and focused way, quite literally, upholds the physical structure we see before us. As more of us awaken to the truth about the origins and purpose of money and our own innate value—the truth about this false sense of power—our once revered structures tumble as they reveal unsteady foundations. Money as we know it today will topple along with this shift. It's nothing to fear; all that isn't built on love is already showing that it will have to leave as our society evolves. Destruction is a natural and much-needed piece of our continued growth and evolution. All we have to do is simply look at our changing seasons to see that death brings about rebirth, growth, and a renewed sense of hope come springtime. And because of this, the way we've been conditioned as a society to work with, interact with, and use money in the present will not be what is taken into the future with us.

As the conditioning around money has evolved throughout history, it has continued to shift the personal, energetic foundation on which we hold our connection to money—our unique Money Design. Money was a revolutionary but rather simple object, one that likely didn't have a very significant effect on the first generation that used it to replace their bartering practices. Once it gained importance, a singular focus, became an object of much attention, and could be yielded against others, these increasingly energetic entanglements to money were formed.

When we look at our individual connection to money—that is, the way that we interact, perceive, and connect with money—we see that it's influenced heavily by this history, society, and our family of origin. These pieces create the history in which our conditioning was set before we even exited our mothers' wombs. This foundation—both practical and energetic—will be explored further in the next chapter along with how our family of origin also forms the foundation of our relationship to money within our Money Design.

CHAPTER 3:
EXPLORING YOUR
MONEY DESIGN

*"Our life is shaped by our mind
for we become what we think."*
-Buddha

Our foundational connection to money, our unique Money Design, is created before we enter this world and continues to develop during our formative childhood years. Like a blueprint, our Money Design acts as a map for how and why you do what you do with money. Your Design is meant to evolve, to change. Bringing awareness to it and discovering tools to work with it are key to shifting your financial reality and the way in which you move forward into living a truly fulfilled life without the pursuit of money being the focus that leads the way.

Your Money Design can't be seen with the naked eye. It encompasses the unseen, energetic pieces of your connection or relationship to money. It's below the surface, tucked away within your subconscious mind and your body. Having a visual of what I'm referring to is helpful before we dive into the specifics. When imagining your Money Design, call up the image of fascia, the connective tissue that encloses muscles within your body. Imagine a body with the muscular system showing and imagine the fascia that surrounds it all. From head to toe, throughout our entire body there is fascia running through us. The fascia can become restricted, causing mobility issues within the body. Many things can create these restrictions within the tissue: traumatic experiences, inflammatory responses, and physical injuries or manipulations. Your Money Design works similarly. Imagine it runs throughout your entire body and it also can cause restrictions of movement, of energy flow. These restrictions could have been with you since your creation or could have been inflicted during an experience in your childhood or beyond. Either way, the restriction is there within your Design, creating a less than stellar flow of energy through your body.

What does energy flow have to do with money? Money is energy, just as all things are energy. When we get down to the subatomic level of everything around us, nothing is actually formed. We are all, to put it simply, moving pieces of energy. And when there is a restriction on an energetic level, there is a restriction in the physical level that we can see, hear, taste, and feel. To understand how energy matters when it comes to why we do what we do with money, and why our Money Design creates our outer financial reality, we must discuss the Law of Correspondence.

The Law of Correspondence is a Universal Law that states, "as within so without, as above so below." Meaning that our outer world, our external and concrete financial reality is a direct result of what is occurring in our inner world: what is being directed by our Money Design. Everything that we see and experience in our day-to-day lives is a mirror. What we see is mirroring back our thoughts, beliefs, and feelings around money (which is also why our emotional triggers or reactions are such important pieces in our Money

Design puzzle). This intangible concept is the basis for understanding why our Money Design is a key component when we want to shift our financial reality. If we aren't willing to accept that our inner reality affects our outer reality, the mirrors we're being shown won't be useful on this journey of growth. Let's look at this a bit differently by imagining that your current financial situation and life is like a movie projector, and you can see your reality playing out in front of you. The film reel is your Money Design, your subconscious thoughts, beliefs, and conditioning around money. Each belief is showcased by a specific frame on the reel, and each lies within your "internal world." Your external world—your bank account, income, debt balances, etc.—are being projected out on the screen in front of you. Now you can try to change out the screen, update it to the newest model, even clean it. But no matter what you do to the screen (the external), you will not be able to change what ultimately "plays" without going to the root of the issue, what's stored on the film reel.

My intention over the course of this book is to take you through the very real, unseen components required to shift your relationship to money—the reels of film that are creating the patterned reality you see before you when it comes to money, fulfillment, and how you believe you derive power. We deconstruct these components so that you can access and embody your innate power, instead of money being a condition around accessing it. Unconsciously, many of us find ourselves on the never-ending hamster wheel of more: more money, more things, more clients, more time. We look for the external markers that we believe will lead us to the fulfillment we are searching for, when in reality, the external world will never truly fulfill our internal longing.

You might have heard that more money equals more power, and as you look at politicians, wealthy business owners, or entertainers it seems to be true. But we've all heard the fable of the wealthy person who has everything money can buy, but still remains unhappy or lonely; or the lottery winners who practically give the money away because they can't seem to hang onto it and note that they surprisingly felt happier once it was gone and life returned to "normal." And no, the moral of these stories isn't that money is evil, far from it. Money is a wonderful tool we can use to support ourselves in this life and I don't believe there can or should be a cap on how much you allow yourself to receive or what you use it for. The moral of the story is this: we innately know that money doesn't buy happiness, it can't buy fulfillment. So, why do we believe that amassing more of it can provide power and the fulfillment that we think will come along with it?

I hope we can agree that everything in this world has a physical, tangible reality while also an unseen, illusive perspective or form. If we're looking at our outer financial reality as a snapshot in time, and if we are in agreement that the Law of Correspondence is in fact reality, then we have to assume that your financial reality is a direct result of your internal world. We're going to assume that your financial reality does not look like anybody else's, even your sibling(s) or parent(s). You have your own unique set of experiences, lenses through which you view life, so we can assume that your internal map and your Money Design is unique to you. These pieces and parts are dictating what you see in your bank account and your financial portfolio as well as how you feel emotionally about what's in front of you.

We can look at your Money Design as a receiving channel: the ways in which you receive money, support, and resources in your life. When we think about your Money Design carrying restrictions, not allowing the full flow of energy to move through your body, we can imagine that your Money Design appears like connective tissue (fascia). This connective tissue is running throughout your body, restricted in certain areas (which mirror limiting beliefs related to money and decrease the flow of energy), and is shaping the way that you currently allow yourself to receive money. The restrictions that are within your receiving channels are slowing down the energetic flow, knotting the channel, making it harder to allow in the resources you desire because of limiting beliefs.

These restrictions aren't permanent, they can be shifted, but it often takes awareness and tools to be able to dive into this unseen, energetic level to do so. And when you're able to pull in energetic tools to release the restrictions within your Design, your receiving channels straighten out in a sense. They widen. They open up, making it easier for you to allow in the money, resources, and support you need to move forward toward what you desire. As we established, money is energy. Everything is energy and our energy leads our interactions, one hundred percent of the time. As you address and shift the root of the restrictions within your Money Design, you are quite literally opening up the receiving channels within your body and ultimately the world you see around you, shifting the way and frequency that you are comfortable receiving money.

When it comes to receiving, our logical minds will ask us: how can we *not* be comfortable receiving money? We all want money, and more of it. We all want to be supported; who wants to struggle and suffer? Well, the truth is, if you have not yet received what it is you desire, there is a part of you that is not comfortable in receiving it. Your brain might scream that I'm wrong, this is crazy, of course you want what you desire and fully believe that you are comfortable in receiving it. But the Law of Correspondence tells us that you're not. Your body tells a different story.

When we get to the root of why your body is not comfortable receiving in the way you would like to, often it comes down to worthiness and safety. Do you truly feel deserving of receiving what you desire? Worthy to receive it now, as you are, with no changes? And does it feel safe to expand outside your comfort zone in this way? Does receiving what it is you desire threaten your survival in a subconscious way? These integral pieces are layered within your Money Design, showing you all the ways that you aren't currently comfortable receiving. As we continue, we'll break down why your body would react in this way and why it feels so hard to shift your ingrained habits and patterns when you're focusing solely on action. But first, let's dive into the nuts and bolts of your Money Design, and then come back to these layers and talk about how and why they're present in your body.

When we're looking at the way that your body is designed to operate, interact, and engage with money, we're looking at your Money Design. By this, I refer to the intricate, energetic web, unseen to the naked eye, that is dictating what you are comfortable receiving at any given moment. So, what is it composed of? Let's break it down into two major pieces and then in the next chapter we'll explore them in more detail.

1. *Your beliefs about money and how you believe you will receive it.*

This means what you believe to be true about the construct of money and in what ways you are comfortable receiving it: the rules in which your body abides by when it comes to receiving. These beliefs come from lived experiences, the environments in which you live now and in the past, and the society in which you were raised. One example of a belief about money and how it affects what you receive: a belief that time equals money and to receive money (in any amount) you need to exchange your hours (in some shape or form) for it. The amount of effort that correlates with the dollar received in this "rule" would vary widely depending on the individual and their Money Design.

2. *Ancestral patterns that you have inherited as your own.*

Ancestral patterns represent beliefs about money that were inherited from your genetic family line. Just like you might inherit knickknacks from your grandparents, you're also inheriting their behaviors around money as you're formed in the womb. The good news? When you bring awareness to them, and utilize the energetic tools, you can shift these patterns at the root.

Within these two overarching components of your Money Design is another piece woven throughout: emotions. When we dive into the beliefs or conditioning you received or created (typically as a child) or inherited ancestrally within the next few chapters, we'll also be talking about an emotional component. The emotional component wrapped within is what is keeping you tied to this belief, the glue that is keeping you feeling tied to a similar pattern that you see with money. This stuck emotional imprint is energetically stored inside your body, oftentimes surfacing when you are in a triggering situation; the trauma brings this emotional imprint back to the forefront in your body. This component is vital to understand and work with when it comes to shifting your financial reality and discovering your key to innate fulfillment and true wealth.

When we look at these pieces that comprise your Money Design, they create the energetic vibration that is mapping why you do what you do with money. Every experience, thought, or action you take is run through this Design, along with your subconscious programming to decide how to react. It's not a conscious realization. Until you bring awareness to it, it's something that you believe to be true because it has always been your truth. Until you can step outside and look at it for what it is, it will not change. Your current reality and the continued actions that you take, stem from your Design. This contributes to how much money and support you receive, in which ways you allow yourself to receive it, and so much more.

Your current Money Design determines your financial reality, at any given moment. We all make choices, all day every day. Even the choices we believe we are "thinking through" and are coming from a place of free will, are still being run through our subconscious programming where our Money Design lies. Over the next few chapters we'll be diving into each aspect I discussed of your Money Design and how these layers can present themselves within your body before moving onto how and why deconstructing them is necessary on your path to inner fulfillment, true wealth, and power.

CHAPTER 4:
THE TRUTH
ABOUT MONEY

*"When a flower doesn't bloom,
you fix the environment in
which it grows, not the flower."*
-Alexander Den Heijer

In this chapter, we're going to dive deeper into one of the components of your Money Design—your beliefs about money and what you believe to be true about receiving it—and touch on the truth about money.

Before we dive in deeper, let's explore the difference between patterns and beliefs. Webster's Dictionary defines a pattern as "a reliable sample of traits, acts, tendencies, or other observable characteristics of a person, group, or institution."[1] Why we do what we do with money is a result of ingrained patterns in our bodies. These patterns influence our spending habits, saving tendencies, even our typical working habits. These habitual things that we do in sum can easily show us what we're doing with money. Let's talk about patterns first. An overarching pattern that I see frequently with clients is not truly understanding where and how money is being spent.

---

1   Merriam-Webster Dictionary, "Definition of PATTERN," Merriam-webster.com, 2019, https://www.merriam-webster.com/dictionary/pattern

The pattern might be habitual spending when it comes to eating out: running through the drive-thru for coffee and breakfast, ordering takeout for supper more often than not, without truly understanding how much you're spending or if you might be overspending (especially for a fixed income). In addition to what I'll refer to as "blind" spending, it is also followed by a consistent avoidance of looking at "the numbers." Not checking your account balance until absolutely necessary, not understanding how much you truly spend and in what categories, and a refusal to sit down and get intimate with your finances until absolutely necessary. Underlying this pattern is an emotional need and belief that is creating discomfort in not being able to face this financial reality. This creates a pattern of spending that (whether real or not) feels like overspending, followed by a discomfort in not knowing if you are okay financially, and topped off with a refusal to sit down and look. The emotional component reinforces this cycle, and eventually when you sit down to face the music, the pressure releases from your body, the emotional component shifts, and you relax having faced the reality of your situation. Only you subconsciously desire to experience this pattern (and emotional rollercoaster) all over again. The underlying belief and need to experience this cycle is unique for each person experiencing it, whether it's because it's a familiar cycle that they witnessed with a parent or caregiver, or because they don't feel deserving of managing money in the first place and tend to avoid the responsibility at all costs.

Underlying the easily accessible patterns, are the beliefs that are prompting these habits. After looking at an example of common patterns, let's look at two examples of common overarching beliefs: 1) time equals money, and 2) that some form of struggle or effort is required to create cash inflow.

Believing that time equals money keeps you within your own energetic limit of how much you are comfortable receiving in exchange for the time you have available. This works on the belief that our ability to receive is directly correlated to how much time we have to expend towards the outcome, leaving most of us short as we have finite time. Depending on your "energetic income ceiling," if you are working with this belief in place, you will reach a point where you no longer want to expend effort in order to receive more money. That limit is different for everyone, but we all have a finite number of hours in the day. In this example, you can look at it like an equation. Time spent = income generated, so what happens when you want to increase the income while simultaneously refusing to increase the time? Things start falling apart. This often feels like you're procrastinating, avoiding and not showing up in a way that you desire, which can feel frustrating and can often breed self-judgment. And when you're in this place, it's often because you are working with this belief (or equation) running within your Money Design. You desire more, but your body does not want to physically expend more effort to feel worthy of receiving it. So, we either push through, leading to physical burnout, or we back off and ultimately settle for less. Your body is in misalignment to what you desire and you'll see the effects one way or another.

The second belief I frequently see show up for clients is that struggle, or effort, is required to create wealth, or receive money. Oftentimes this leads to creating an environment where our business, profession, or relationships feel harder than needed to in order to satisfy this belief. Because we need to prove our worthiness to receive, working hard is one way to satisfy our belief in struggle. Who else has heard the phrase "the fruits of your labor" or listened to a family member reminisce about a particularly laborious profession with fondness and pride at a "hard day's work"? Struggle doesn't have to be a necessary component to receive money or create wealth. Our society often romanticizes these struggle-to-triumph stories, but this reality is not true across the board. There are people who received money, and created wealth, without it needing to be hard. Do we often need some form of intention and effort to create? Yes, but that doesn't mean that struggle has to be a necessary component within.

There are no rules when it comes to receiving, other than making sure your body believes that you can have whatever it is you desire. Typical habits that can appear when the above beliefs are running behind the scenes are: never creating space for rest, self-care, or a time-out; always believing that you don't have the time to rest, to take a break, or to slow down and re-evaluate; and feeling like your schedule, business, or life is running you, rather than you running it.

Patterns like these, and many others, are fueled by our beliefs. Most of our beliefs were picked up in our formative childhood years from family and the conditioning received from the society we were raised within. Although these patterns are likely imitations of what was modeled to us as children, they are also related to the beliefs that underlie them. These beliefs are held in our bodies and the easiest way to bring awareness to them is to pay attention to the patterns that they encourage. Behind every pattern, especially an unconscious pattern or pattern we are trying to shift, is a belief that is anchoring it into your body making it feel harder to shift.

Until we can expose the root, get underneath the patterns to the beliefs and conditioning, it can be hard to truly shift these patterns in the long term. When you're able to shift patterns on a permanent level, it's a clear indicator that your Money Design has changed internally, that a belief has shifted. This begs the question, why can't we take our easily recognizable patterns and shift them to a pattern that feels more supportive of reaching our goals? Why do we have to dig down to the root belief?

As I mentioned in the Introduction, we can look at this concept through the lens of clearing weeds or diseased bushes from your garden. Would you simply cut the top off and expect the problem to be solved? No, of course not. You would dig up the dirt around it and shovel all the way into the Earth to pull up every last piece of the diseased root to ensure the safety and health of the other plants in your garden. Let's use this analogy to look at another pattern to help us explore this concept. A sometimes common pattern is hiding purchases from a partner, family member, or friend; and/or telling "little white lies" about prices. This pattern, or habit, is the above-the-ground weed that has taken over the garden or flower bed. We can see its gnarly leaves and body snaking its way through the beautiful, planted landscape. Within this scenario, the person telling the "little white lie" can intellectually realize that they are lying or hiding. Oftentimes a behavior like this comes so naturally that the person doing it might not even understand why it feels almost reflexive to lie, or to hide. Even if this person has not themselves experienced a situation where they were shamed or yelled at about purchasing something, it is a reflexive reaction likely to avoid pain and remain "safe." This person might try to stop themselves when they become aware of the pattern but can't seem to completely shift the desire to hide.

When we think about this above-the-ground weed, intuitively we know that we can't simply take some garden shears and chop the weed off where it can be viewed above the Earth. We have to go deeper and pull it up by the roots. And conversely in this example, we likely can't force anyone into fessing up to everything, telling the truth about prices, and "outing" everything that has been hidden because it doesn't feel safe. For someone who has been practicing this pattern, and more than likely witnessing this pattern for decades, it can feel very uncomfortable and even fearful to the body to think of operating in any other way. Forcing themselves to change likely would not hold long term because they're not addressing the deeply rooted issue. So, then what do we do?

We have to go deeper. When we look at the gardening analogy, our beliefs are the below-the-ground pieces of this weed that we can't see with the naked eye. Simply attacking our patterns will leave you vulnerable to the pattern returning in the same way (or to something that looks and feels similar). In this example it leaves the person facing temporary discomfort that eventually gets masked again with the same, or similar pattern to return the body to a sense of "safe" normalcy. In this case, the conscious realization of the "hiding" pattern is the awareness, and it triggers an invitation to go deeper and see what belief underneath this pattern is fueling the need to create coping behaviors that are masking the deeply rooted belief.

Let's take another real-life pattern and dissect it while looking at the difference between patterns and beliefs. No matter what your income level is or has been in the past, you still find a way to spend almost all the excess income you receive outside your monthly expenses. Whether you make $2,000 or $20,000 a month, you manage to spend it all by the end of the month or pretty close to it. This leaves you wondering what happened to the money and why you weren't able to save or divert some cash toward a goal. Of course, the money didn't just disappear. It was spent in various ways throughout the month in—likely—a very patterned way. Maybe you like to give away money, buy things for other people, shop online; maybe you like to go out for drinks with friends. Whatever your patterns are, no matter the income that comes in, these ingrained habits kick up or dial back depending on the income level. Regardless of your income level, you are left at the end of the day with little or nothing to show for it. This is the pattern.

Underneath the pattern—which includes many spending habits—there are beliefs and conditioning that are propping up the habits that are leading to no excess cash at the end of the month. If you were to try to attack the patterns or habits to shift them, it might look like creating a budget, cutting up your credit cards, downloading a spending tracker. Anyway you cut it, it will likely feel physically and emotionally restrictive. The person with this pattern is likely beating themselves up, "Why can't I just stop spending?" or, "Why can't I figure this out?" Some people within this pattern will be able to keep themselves in this restrictive phase (i.e. eating ramen for a month instead of going out to eat) and see a surplus at the end of the month. But this isn't sustainable. And this system is only successful (in this example success is defined as seeing a surplus) when you stay in the struggle, meaning there is an underlying belief that allows you to create the surplus *if* you are doing [insert restrictive habit here]. This ties in with the belief that we discussed at the beginning of the chapter, creating a need for struggle in order to receive.

When we're talking about shifting your financial reality, you can see that attacking the pattern is often the hard route. And usually it doesn't result in a long-lasting shift if not also coupled with the deeper (under the pattern) belief work.

Below the pattern lies the belief that is figuratively propping up the pattern. In the example above, this is the reason why your body is actually not comfortable in having excess cash at the end of the month. It might be okay receiving in large amounts (depending on what income level you're currently receiving), but it isn't okay with having the surplus and moving forward differently which would allow you to reach certain financial goals. The root beliefs will vary depending on your specific situation, but most commonly in this example it comes down to worthiness or safety. The belief tells you are worthy at a base level to receive what it is you desire, or tells you that it's safe in order for you to receive at a level above where you are currently. This is especially true when life feels good and easy in certain areas, when you've reached the income you've been desiring, making headway, and yet find yourself still unable to create excess cash at the end of the month, still being unable to create movement toward a new form of wealth which might look like: a retirement fund, investment portfolio, paying off your commercial debt, or upgrading your lifestyle.

If you've decided to attack the pattern rather than going to the root, you might find that you're able to create a surplus because you are struggling in the process. And if you believe you're not worthy of receiving when life feels too easy, you will be able to create a surplus when forcing yourself into a restrictive environment and creating stress, struggle, and overwhelm.

When we go through life attempting to remedy our patterns, you can see how we end up short. We live out the same patterns on repeat, typically the ones we were exposed to as children, simply because the root belief hasn't been addressed yet.

That's why (for many of us) we can do all the budgeting, tracking, affirmations, and money mindset work we can get our hands on but still not see the shifts we desire. Why? Because they don't go deep enough to address the root cause of why we're doing what we do with money in an unconscious environment. Bringing conscious awareness to not only our financial reality, but our entire lives, is crucial to ushering in real, sustainable change. To experience and uncover your unique key to innate power and wealth, you must be willing and open to shifting the world within you. Our current reality is created due to our current thoughts, beliefs, and environment.

Within our current thoughts, beliefs, and environment are the old systems that are designed to keep us tied to the beliefs that: power is outside of you, and in order to access it, you need to accumulate lots of money to wield said power. These beliefs need to be deconstructed and deprogrammed in order to move into a space where we can access our innate power and create wealth and fulfillment. We do this through conscious awareness of our patterns, which helps us to move deeper into conscious awareness of our beliefs. This intentional work isn't always easy. Most of us have been hardwired to move unconsciously through life, accepting things at their face value, not questioning, or probing as to why.

This awareness as you dive in or dive more deeply into your relationship to money begets a great awakening. An awakening that once the covers are pulled back, can never be undone. That's the beauty of waking up in this way: there is no possible way of going back to sleep. As we dig into the layers and layers of beliefs sitting underneath our patterns that lead us to living life in a way that feels disempowering and unfulfilling, we begin to question why. Why is it that most people seem to be moving through life in this way that keeps us from living a fulfilled life due to our unconscious beliefs? That a small group of people have access to this information and the truth about money? Why do some have the ability to create and receive wealth and wield influence over others? Why are we playing this game and why can't we all create our own sense of fulfillment through an internal lens?

We talked about the real truth about money, its physical construct, and what it was intended to be used for. But what has it turned into? A tool that is amassed and wielded by the few to attempt to direct the many. We don't have to look far to find beliefs that "money is the root of all evil" and that "billionaires should be proportionately taxed to give to the many," but I believe this is shifting personal responsibility away from those who are deemed to not "have enough." It is akin to the concept, "give a man a fish, and he will be fed for a day but teach a man to fish, and he will be fed for life." Why aren't we teaching others that they are quite literally making decisions about and with their money that don't serve them or their goals? While financial literacy is incredibly important and necessary, what about emotional intelligence when it comes to money? What about understanding how our actions are derived subconsciously and how we can work with our emotional triggers? If we truly want change and comfort for all, the answer lies beneath financial handouts and within showing others that it's okay to take money off the pedestal and return the power you've given it back within yourself. This attachment to this false idol, money, is allowing us to stay in a disempowered state, keeping money at arm's length as we deem ourselves not worthy.

This awakening isn't for the faint of heart. You might have already experienced a spiritual awakening of sorts, or are amid one, so you might know the feeling: the confusion, unsteadiness, and discomfort. There's a financial awakening to be had not only on an individual level, but on a collective level as well. One where we can step out of the illusionary web that our modern-day financial system has woven around us. To see it for what it is: a construct. One that we are willingly a part of. But nevertheless, we can decide to be willing participants that realize it's time for change. And that change starts within us, all of us. There is no system that can withstand a mass awakening to its misalignment. As we shift collectively, our systems have no choice but to be faced, destroyed, and rebuilt in accordance, as we energetically participate in the co-creation of this Universe and all of its components.

I don't believe it's an accident or a coincidence that we are programmed to behave, chase, and place money on a pedestal. When we step back and look at the material things we desire, the lives that we desire to live, there's absolutely nothing wrong with wanting to accumulate money to fund that experience. It's the energy behind why, the energy behind the chase, the desire, the need for more. It's the understanding of whether or not we are desiring from a conscious place of awareness, or an unconscious desire to act on a belief that isn't ours to begin with.

As you untangle your relationship to money, you'll discover more about yourself. You'll releasing the beliefs or patterns that weren't yours to begin with and that are no longer necessary as you move into a new chapter of thriving. Where inner fulfillment, true what our ancestors endured. Scientific studies have shown the link and probability that traumatic events are passed down to descendants.[1] This has led me to the realization—from witnessing firsthand with myself and hundreds of clients—that we are heavily influenced, not only by our parents' genes and DNA, but by their very real and lived experiences around money and that these affected us before we were even a twinkle in their eye.

From a metaphysical standpoint this is clear. When we look at the experience that created the traumatic event, the person who went through the event or who is carrying a trauma from witnessing the event has strong emotional ties from the experience. If these events and the correlating emotions were not processed and allowed to move through the body—both physically and energetically—then the body will hold onto this restriction. That is, until it's able to process and release the emotional resonance (a.k.a. perception) from this event to allow the energy to flow freely. In strong emotional events where we were not detached from or neutral to our emotional states, or did not have the tools to help our bodies process the shock, we were changed physiologically. It's easy to see how this changed body and its epigenetic traits would then be passed along to our offspring. This leaves our offspring feeling the effects, unbeknownst to them, of the original trauma in which they had no physical part, resulting in confusion as to why they innately react in certain ways to situations.

How does this happen? According to Shaili Jain, M.D., a clinical associate professor of Psychiatry and Behavioral Sciences at the Stanford University School

---

1   Martha Henriques, "Can the Legacy of Trauma Be Passed Down the Generations?", Bbc.com (BBC Future, 2019), https://www.bbc.com/future/article/20190326-what-is-epigenetics

of Medicine, "Trauma often represents the violation of all we hold to be dear and sacred. Such events are often simply too terrible to utter aloud, and hence they often become unspeakable. [W]hen these traumatic thoughts and memories remain unspeakable or unthinkable for too long, they often impede our brain's natural process of recovery after trauma. They become stuck points that inhibit the mental reintegration that is needed for healing to occur." This creates a literal physical effect on natural hormone rhythms, organ functions, and more, leading us to the belief that our body does in fact store trauma in a physical manner.[2]

On top of the genetic component, our family of origin also contributes to and influences our thoughts, emotions, and beliefs surrounding money after we are born. When we are young, the experiences we witness, the conversations we overhear, and the emotional highs and lows that most of us experience within our households shape our foundational relationship to money: our Money Design. These leave imprints on our bodies, shape our subconscious patterning, and solidify knee-jerk responses in all areas of our lives. Since money and our finances are a key component in much of our lives, it's easy to see how beneficial it is to dive into healing work through this influential lens.

Along with epigenetics—soaking up this familial conditioning like a sponge when we're young—we also bring in the human race's history with money to add another layer. Let's explore that next.

---

2   Stephanie Eckelkamp, "Can Trauma Really Be 'Stored' In The Body?", mindbodygreen.com (2020) https://www.mindbodygreen.com/articles/can-trauma-be-stored-in-body

have two cars in the driveway. Debt that allows you to obtain this lifestyle is acceptable debt.

9. Be humble and grateful for what money you do have, not everyone is as lucky as you are.

10. Work hard to earn your money, don't be lazy. You must work to receive.

As you read through these societal beliefs, how many of them resonate with you? Did other societal or institutional rules float into your awareness? Stop to think about how these concepts and ideas relate to your real, physical life. It is important as you deconstruct your relationship to money to uncover what's running within your Money Design.

Bringing awareness into your everyday life helps you make a new choice, or the same choice, intentionally. New choices create new realities. Until we bring awareness to the rules that are subconsciously governing our body and our actions forward with money, we can't change them. Literally. Our inner world directs our outer world as we discussed within the Law of Correspondence. Until we are ready to dive deeper within and question why we believe the way we believe, our outer world is going to stay relatively the same. Hence, we see the same money patterns play out month after month, year after year. Until you can look at the underlying emotions or patterns behind your current financial situation and the patterns that created it, you likely won't be able to grow out of it. Sure, things will shift and shuffle around, but at the root of it, you'll likely be experiencing the same emotional patterns just in a different situation. You will be running in circles, continuing to find yourself back where you started. Let's illustrate this with another example.

It's January; a new year, a fresh start. You've decided you're going to make this year count financially. "Crush" the debt, create an emergency savings account, and master your relationship to money.

What do most of us do when we create new goals that we want to achieve? We create some type of plan to help us get there. In this case, you create a budget, download an app to track your purchases and alert you when you've reached certain spending limits (i.e. all above the ground actions when looking at pulling out the diseased plant example in Chapter 4). You're excited, on a high, thinking about how this time you are going to once and for all destroy these patterns. No more feast or famine for you, stretching your last penny until payday. You're going to have a surplus, a savings account, zero debt, and control of your financial reality.

As you can foresee, this high of planning, hoping, wishing is likely going to lead to a "low." Which begs the question, why do so many people experience this high to low, feast and famine pattern with money?

When we look at our lives, if we are living unconsciously within them, we are consistently recreating similar patterns and entering into relationships that recreate emotional experiences from our childhood. It's a psychological safety mechanism. If you grew up in a home that was consistently in feast and famine cycles, whether they came in the form of money, emotional or physical attention, or otherwise, you will unconsciously recreate similar highs and lows as you head into adulthood. That is, until you begin to bring awareness to the pattern and consciously work to change it.

Working specifically with this financial goal, why do most resolutions, goals, diets, etc. fail? Because the actions taken are ninety-nine percent surface level. They don't go below the physical actions when it comes to creating long-lasting change. *Trying to get rid of the weed by only removing what you can see at the surface.* They don't delve into why you desire to spend more than you know you'll bring in; why spending makes you feel good and serves as a coping mechanism to avoid traumatic emotional experiences; or why you actually—on a subconscious level—feel better in lack or scarcity due to how you were raised.

So, when we talk about our outer world being a direct reflection of our inner world, it's easy to see through an example. If in our outer world we are experiencing feast and famine at each month's end as we wait for payday, we can take a look and see where in our inner world that pattern is stemming from. What belief, or familial or ancestral conditioning, is contributing to that? And why? The patterns in our outer reality are the perfect place to begin bringing awareness and diving into our inner world which is where the true shifts begin to occur.

Let's dive deeper into how our relationship or connection to money is formed. Ancestral trauma, family of origin patterns or conditioning, and societal conditioning, these pieces carry the weight in how we move forward in our current connection to money, a.k.a. why our current reality looks the way it does and why it feels difficult to shift no matter how hard we try. We can look at these pieces as instructions or codes as we move forward in life; they are the operating system that our body is working from.

Let's take another real-life example as to how these codes create real-life action in our lives: let's say you want to purchase a new home. The search for your home, where you look, the price range you look at, the home you eventually purchase (or don't purchase) is all run through your subconscious filters (a.k.a. beliefs). Take the example of a couple looking to purchase a house for their growing family. Now, we'll look at some filters that the house purchasing process will run through when, for the sake of simplicity, we take the example of a suburban home in the United States of America. This is assuming that these beliefs are still unconscious to this couple, allowing these filters to run unbeknownst to them.

- Did both, or one, of their families of origin affirm the "American dream" (i.e. suburban home, white picket fence and two cars in the garage)? Is that something that was touted as a badge of honor or something to strive to attain?
- If so, do they aspire to please their parent(s) or care-giver(s) for external validation? Or have they been comfortable making independent choices without feeling the need for their choices to be validated?
- Depending on these answers, they will either be drawn toward a suburban lifestyle or repelled by it.
- Did either of them grow up in a household that lived beyond their means? Was money always tight for their parent(s) or caregiver(s) because they overex-tended themselves?
- Are they driven to not repeat the same patterns they witnessed when they were young and have some awareness?

The price range they are comfortable purchasing in will be influenced by their answers. Of course, we are simplifying the process and taking all other factors out of the equation. But this gives us an overview of how our actions are run through our filters, and how each filter is influenced based upon our awareness of it. Clearly, the less aware you are of the patterns and conditioning that are lying below the surface, the more likely it is you will create and continue to repeat what has already been done. Meaning, you will find yourself living a similar life to your parent(s) or caregiver(s), or one that is highly regarded and validated by them, even if it's highly dysfunctional and nothing that your conscious brain wants. While also repeating similar experiences and patterns year over year, you'll end up living a relatively constant life with not much change.

While the idea that our connection to money is created and affected by these items appears simple, it's a complex web to unravel. To help us bring clarity to why these beliefs affect our outward reality requires a conversation about quantum physics.

Science has proven what many of us intuitively know: everything is energy. And just as we are a part of the vast Universe, we are also energy. Always moving, vibrating in our unique way. From these discoveries made within quantum physics, one potential revelation is the finding that we, as human observers, are creating our own physical reality.[3] Although it has been proven that nothing is truly physical, we're all immaterial energy waves floating within the constraints of our current place and time. What many intuitively know— that we create our reality—was found to be true by scientists. Our Universe is a "mental construction" and we are active participants. There are scientific studies at our fingertips which conclude that our consciousness can be used to alter our physical, material world. Our thoughts, emotions, and experiences shape the very reality that is in front of us at any given time. Our inner world affects and directs our outer reality.

With this logic, our thoughts, emotions, beliefs are quite literally creating the financial reality that we see before us in our everyday lives. If nothing is truly physical, this life is a mental construction in which we are active participants. Can you see the innate power we

3   Arjun Walia. "Nothing Is Solid & Everything Is Energy – Scientists Explain The World of Quantum Physics." Collective Evolution, September 27, 2014, https://www.collective-evolution.com/2014/09/27/this-is-the-world-of-quantum-physics-nothing-is-solid-and-everything-is-energy/

have over creating our financial reality? And not just our financial reality, but our entire world?

When we can bring awareness to what's lying below the surface, we are accessing an innate power that we didn't realize existed. It's been slowly picked away over the creation of money. And while it's easy to read and say that we are the co-creators of our lives, before we can embody this reality there's a lot of baggage that needs to be sifted through. This is where the process of deconstructing our connection to money comes in—to make sure that we have the right plane ticket, the right baggage (a.k.a. it belongs to us, not our ancestors) before we hop on that plane and attempt to fly to where we want to go (our desires and goals, and ensuring they are truly ours to begin with and not built on top of beliefs and conditioning that are not ours).

This awareness helps us dig beneath the surface for something we can wrap our hands around when we talk about why we do what we do with money, why we see the same patterns play month after month, year after year. No matter how we try and force ourselves to change our habits, we find ourselves right back where we started for good reason. We frankly weren't going deep enough.

And with that in mind, let's go deeper shall we?

Before you move into the next chapter, I invite you to stop and reflect. This is the intentional pause that I alluded to at the beginning of the book. After this chapter, you will find an end of section resource with reflections drawn from the discussion over the last five chapters and a guided visualization to help you access, see, and feel your very own Money Design as it stands currently. After listening to this visualization, I invite you to reflect with the prompts and visualizations listed.

REFLECTION 1: PAUSE - REFLECT - PROCESS

To access your e-course that accompanies this book, enter www.moremoneymorepowerbook.com in your web browser. After entering your e-mail address you will have access to the visualizations and reflection workbooks that were designed to help you deepen the work within these pages. Below are the reflection questions and activities that you can take to deepen the work from Section 1: Chapters 1 through 5. If you'd rather print a workbook to use, you can access it with the above link along with your guided visualizations.

Access the audio recording and guided visualization to support you in connecting with your current Money Design at www.moremoneymorepowerbook.com.

Below are the accompanying reflection questions to help you deepen the work while listening to the recordings or for further support afterward, for Chapters 1 through 5:

1. As you read and reflect on the Law of Correspondence, "as within, so without," can you see how your internal reality and makeup affects what you see outside of yourself? Have you had experiences that paint this belief as true?

_____

_____

_____

_____

_____

_____

_____

2. An important key to deconstructing your current relationship to money is reflecting on how you believe you derive your internal state of fulfillment. Do you believe the key to happiness is more money? That your problems will be solved with more? How so? And if you imagined your bank account balance could increase tenfold right now, how would that change your perception of yourself? Reflecting on these questions will help you to bring awareness to any beliefs that are lying dormant.

_____

_____

_____

_____

_____

_____

_____

3. Patterns vs. Beliefs. Take a moment and list the typical patterns that you see showing up when it comes to money in your day-to-day life? Then, spend time reflecting on them to see if you can attribute them to a specific belief that is supporting them?

_____

_____

_____

_____

_____

_____

4. An important part of this deconstructing work is our openness to change. Change when it comes to shifting your habits, patterns, and beliefs. But also how open you are to the reality that your financial situation can change. Think about a year from now, can you imagine your financial situation as being radically different and what does that difference look like? And how does your body react to this belief? Now change the date to tomorrow, how does your body and comfort level shift?

    _____

    _____

    _____

    _____

    _____

5. When we bring awareness to your foundational relationship to money, we look at the adults present in your life when you were a child. What were your parent(s) or caregiver(s) relationship to money while you were growing up? What were the common themes or patterns you remember witnessing? If accessing childhood memories feels more difficult, look at any patterns or habits that are present for them today. Once you've reflected on this, take a moment and reflect on how these patterns might be affecting you and your habits in your day-to-day financial reality.

    _____

    _____

    _____

    _____

6. What beliefs around money can you see have already shifted over the years, and what do you believe has prompted those shifts?

_____

_____

_____

_____

_____

_____

_____

_____

7. What beliefs around money are you more than ready to leave behind? What do you believe is stopping you from achieving that right here, right now?

_____

_____

_____

_____

_____

_____

_____

_____

_____

8. After going through your reflection questions, let's dive into the Money Design guided visualization. How did your Design feel? What did it look like? Reflect on why you believe those visuals came through, and if you're feeling creative, try drawing or mapping it in a separate journal.

_____

_____

_____

_____

_____

_____

_____

_____

_____

_____

_____

DREAM ON

CHAPTER 6:
THE POWER OF
YOUR DREAM

*"There are some people who
live in a dream world, and there
are some who face reality; and
then there are those who turn
one into the other."*

-Douglas H. Everett

Hopefully by now you can understand why I call wealth an "inside game." Proportionately, when it comes to creating wealth and receiving money, it's not only what you do in the external world, but how your internal world, your Money Design, is structured. And the action that stems from this place will lead you to where you desire to go. Now that we've painted the picture of what your Money Design is, we'll move into the how. How to shift your Money Design. How the awareness and tools you cultivate can help you step into your innate power and wealth from the inside out.

I'm going to go out on a limb and say that most of us desire more money to support us in creating new experiences for ourselves or our family. That's what we want. But what most of us *need* are the tools and information to tap into the power we already hold when it comes to accessing our innate wealth. An embodiment that doesn't come and go as your bank account fills up and empties. Because wealth doesn't equal money. Wealth is a way of being that allows us to experience, achieve, and create from a place that never "needs" and doesn't experience lack. It always trusts. It knows undoubtedly that it will be provided for, provisions will be given.

When it comes to shifting our reality from the inside out, awareness is the first step. It can be easy for us to identify a "problem" (i.e. we need more money or need to pay down our debt) and rush into action, set up the budget, track the spending, cut up our credit card, or do all the things from that article you found called "The 10 Best Ways To Pay Off Debt." But there are messages missed in this knee-jerk instinctual reaction led by our subconscious, causing us to more often than not recreate the same pattern experienced only weeks or months prior. When the "problem" appears before us and we feel a knee-jerk response to act, it's an opportunity to pause. To bring awareness to the situation or the experience you're having and allow a new solution to take its place. Because awareness is beautiful, awareness is necessary, but awareness can only take you so far. Once the awareness of the pattern and habits that recreate the pattern appear, it's time to go deeper.

If you took yourself through the visualization and reflection prompts at the end of Chapter 5, then you can see what a beautiful picture awareness can bring. When it comes to uncovering beliefs we have about money, wealth, worthiness, we can find more if we decide to look. The deconstructing of old programs will likely continue until the day you die—as long as you're focused on growth. There is so much embedded in our current reality and our current society that keeps us living in contrast to the truth. *The truth that you are worthy, now*, along with your flaws, your mistakes, with your current ever-evolving conditions. There is nothing you need to do, be, or give to be worthy of receiving what it is you desire. And as long as you are committed to unlearning and deconstructing your internal programs around money, you will remain on this continuous growth curve as you experience, explore, and learn. Awareness is step one, but it can only take you so far before you find yourself unknowingly repeating the same destructive patterns ad nauseam. Once awareness is brought in, it's time to *go deeper.*

We are often conditioned to stay above the surface, to accept what is in front of us, and to settle for the cards we're dealt. The reality is we all have access to much, much more than we realize. We are capable of much more than we give ourselves credit for. Awareness is the possibility to open ourselves up to the idea that life as we see it now doesn't have to stay this way. You aren't predestined when it comes to your financial future, your profession, your level of happiness. You have the power to decide, regardless of the deck you've been handed. Some decks might have fewer cards than others initially, but I fully believe and have seen that we all have the innate power and will to create the life we desire when we're able to tap into our Money Design and work with what we've been given. And where does it begin? It begins with a dream.

You wouldn't be here, reading this book, if you didn't desire something more than what you currently have. The frequency, the vibration, that this book emits would never have resonated on an unconscious level with you. These words, the activations and exercises within these pages were created to support the dreamers. The visionaries. The wayshowers, who know that they are here for a bigger purpose on this Earth and who wholeheartedly believe that wealth is their birthright. This space between where you are now and where you want to be is the bridge. The bridge that is needed to cross into your new reality, new lifestyle, new experience. Along that bridge there are money beliefs waiting to be deconstructed, and action to be taken outside your current comfort zone. The desire to cross the bridge must be greater than the fear or hesitation that lies in walking that path. Our desire must be greater than our fear if we're to succeed in making progress toward our goals.

I want you to take a moment and dream with me. In a moment, I want you to close your eyes and imagine your dream life. Where would you be living? Who would you be with, if anyone? What would you be doing? And how would you be feeling? Take a moment now—yes, you—close your eyes and allow yourself to pull up that visual in your mind.

Now bring awareness to your body. Take a moment and rub your hands together, take a big deep breath in and out, feeling your whole body shift in response. Bring yourself back to your physicality and deepen your sense of awareness to how your body has reacted to the dreaming you just did. I'm going to guess you feel somewhere on the spectrum of excited, energized, and happy. You brought your body into the emotional state of the future, of your desired future, of where you want to go. Now most of us find that we aren't able to maintain this emotional frequency and state. These feelings, thoughts, visions are quickly replaced with the reality of our very real "now moment," where we don't yet have the beach house, the passport stamped and filled, the sprawling estate. And when we snap back into our reality, oftentimes we feel the discord from being far from that dream. It's a stark reminder that we are not where we want to be and the path or the bridge to get there feels insurmountable. That immediate gut reaction highlights where in our bodies we don't fully believe that the life we desire is something we are capable of receiving. You might have noticed within your body that you felt restriction, or tightness, as you thought about what you wanted versus what you are experiencing currently. The excitement might have been replaced with anxiety or frustration. This all highlights where your body is harboring resistance to receiving what it is you desire and is part of your Money Design. Let's use an example from a client of mine, Sarah (I am sharing with her permission and have changed her personal details).

Sarah is an alternative healthcare practitioner with varied professional certifications, years of experience, and a solid track record of supporting clients and helping them achieve transformational results. She came to me because she couldn't seem to move past a pattern of hers: years of effort, hard work, and consistency within her business that wasn't producing sustainable, steady income for her and her family. She was astounded at the lack of results she was seeing despite her consistent action, effort, and willingness to show up for her clients and her business. She desired to have a thriving business that would create income to consistently support her and her family. Instead, she was seeing spurts of income, dry spells, and results that did not equal the amount of effort she was putting in.

As I do with all clients, we went to her body. We know the body holds the keys, and the messages that we need to identify where shifts must occur so that we can achieve what we desire. And in this case, the desire is to see steady, consistent income that will support her family. Within our first session, once we brought awareness to the pattern and identified what it is she desired, we then went to the body. Through monitoring Sarah's emotional states as we talked, we identified that she was feeling dread, sadness, and being frozen. As we entered a meditative state, after creating a grounded safe space that allowed her to feel comfortable in exploring, we began to examine, with her body leading, where these emotional imprints originated from. She spoke up and immediately said she saw herself in a hallway with her younger sister, listening to her parents fighting in their bedroom late at night. This was a few months to a year before they eventually divorced which changed her family life permanently. That feeling of dread, sadness, and being frozen originated from that moment at age seven. In a way, part of her body was trapped emotionally at that age along with the imprints associated with the event. After diving in further with energetic techniques, we could see that the real fear in moving forward into a consistent, easy, profitable business had everything to do with not wanting to leave her younger sister behind.

Sarah's younger sister struggles deeply as an adult emotionally, physically, financially. And there's a part of Sarah (deep down) that doesn't want to move past this emotional state—away and out of sync with her sister. Even though they're both grown with children of their own, what happened in that hallway and the months after were defining moments for their bodies and Sarah specifically held resistance in her body to the thought of moving past that state. Staying in the struggle when it comes to her business kept her in that underlying emotional state that has repeated itself in various areas of her life over the last few decades. After spending some time continuing to explore Sarah's feelings around needing to be responsible for her sister, staying tied to the family unit, and their emotional imprints, we could move into emotional release work and additional energetic techniques to help her shift her internal state. In the next chapter we will dive deeper into the importance of working with our emotional states when it comes to shifting the awareness that arises so you can create a different financial reality.

For Sarah, there was much relief that came from the realization and release of the emotional imprints stemming from that experience. It has cascaded into her, continuing to dive deeper into the interrelationships with her family of origin and the role she plays within it as she energetically continues to remove herself from her past role. In this case, her body before we had this session was not designed to receive a consistent, steady income because that would have put her "ahead" of her sibling and in discomfort because of it. It would put her far outside her role, which was to be responsible for her and her sister's happiness. A state of struggle felt safer, albeit more uncomfortable to Sarah's subconscious mind because it was where her sister was emotionally. Until the root issue was addressed as to why she felt she was responsible for her sister, and why she was not comfortable in breaking up the family unit on this energetic level, her body would likely never feel comfortable with financial success. That is unless her sister was also working toward successful endeavors that created a fulfilled life, and they could do it together. This gave her the confidence and awareness to not only energetically separate her dreams and her desires from the constructs and limits of her family of origin, but it also gave her great awareness to take with her as she evaluated all of her patterns, her habits, and her ingrained knee-jerk reactions that were stemming from this original pattern.

In this case, the awareness of her pattern—a lot of hard work, effort, and struggle without a corresponding output in terms of money—had been her norm within her business. She was aware that there was a

I know you have a mission, a purpose in this life because we all do. Whether you deem it to be big or small, whether it's on the stage or centered around supporting yourself or your family, it matters equally, nonetheless. You are a powerful creator even if you don't realize it at this moment. But given the knowledge and the tools to strip away and deprogram the conditioning you have around money, you will be able to support yourself as you step into your role in the natural order without needing money to take that first step. Trust that as you continue to move forward in your purpose, cultivating and accessing your God-given gifts and talents, that you are (and will continue to be) supported financially, emotionally, physically. That as you experience, and create, as you play the game here on Earth, that your needs will be met when you believe they'll be met. Because why wouldn't they be?

CHAPTER 7:
MONEY DRAMA-
EMOTIONS AND MONEY

"Healing dysfunctional patterns are more urgent than promotion. When we advance without healing, we take our self-sabotage with us."

-Dr. Thema Bryant-Davis

Before we begin, I want you to sit with what we ended on in Chapter 6—trust. Blind faith that you will be provided for no matter what on a financial, physical, and emotional level. Sit for a moment with this idea, reread the last sentence and pay very close attention to how your body reacts and how you feel. Do thoughts or judgments rise within you reflecting a perceived naivety? Do you want to believe that it's true, but there's a part of your brain that is pulling up memories and experiences that disprove it? Does it create anxiety, frustration, or possibly even excitement anywhere within your body? Take a moment and allow your body to show you how it currently feels about the statement: You are provided for on a financial, physical, and emotional level at all times.

As I've mentioned several times, our emotional states contain important messages for us as we set out to deprogram and deconstruct our relationship to money so that we can create our lives and experiences more easily. Because that's the whole point, right? We want to create, experience, and move toward our goals and dreams, without feeling stuck in a hamster wheel unable to reach them. Deconstructing our programming around money is an important task if we're ready and eager to tap into our innate power and access the wealth that's afforded to all of us, without waiting for money to show up and give us the right to do so. And the keys to doing this often lay within our emotional states. Moving into emotional neutrality with money takes it off the pedestal we have it on and brings it back down to Earth. Meaning, we need to look at the emotional states within our body that are wrapped up in our feelings, thoughts, attitudes, and experiences with money to recreate a level playing field. To return it to its natural state: a tool.

A neutral emotional connection to money doesn't mean that you're ignoring your feelings or bypassing them in any way. In fact, connecting and listening to your emotional body is one of the most important things we can do on this path of growth. We are here to recognize our innate value as souls to help us move forward in confidence. When we can do this, we're able to attract the resources needed to see our visions through to completion, to increase our fulfillment, and to rediscover and embody our innate power. In this mission our emotional body is key. It's important to work *with* our emotions in shifting and releasing our outdated programming and beliefs around money, rather than pushing them aside as unhelpful. Diving in through our emotional states supports us in embracing the feelings that arise around the different aspects of our financial situations and experiences, and *shifts* our current ability to receive.

Contrary to the "good vibes only" outlook, I believe there are no "bad" emotions. The reverse is also true, there are no emotions inherently better than others. Of course, there are emotions that most of us enjoy feeling more than others, but that doesn't discount the validity of all emotions across the spectrum. All emotions are messages; they aren't inherently good or bad. They're guideposts showing us what's happening on an internal level, underneath the surface of our bodies that might need attention and a closer look. When we're experiencing what I'll call "lower-vibration emotions" like anger, fear, or guilt—keeping in mind that I don't mean "bad" emotions—we are being presented an opportunity to dig deeper and not to bypass, push away, or focus solely on "high-vibration emotions" (like joy, ecstasy, and happiness). This simple shift in awareness helps to recognize that all emotions are guideposts. And when we can look at our emotional states and triggers (specifically for our low-vibration emotions), we see them as invitations to dig deeper and explore. When it comes to money, there might not be a bigger emotional trigger out there for us to learn from. Not because money is more important than other areas of our lives, but because of the intense programming we have embedded around money and the deep-seated beliefs we carry that point to money as validation of our worthiness. Coupled with the fact that money is pervasive in our lives, it gives us a huge opportunity to not only shift our financial reality but so many other aspects of our lives, as we deconstruct and heal these parts of ourselves.

Let's take an example to illustrate. When we experience a financial loss, surprise, or even upset—for example receiving an unexpected $10,000 tax bill in the mail—we know it will likely cause an emotional reaction. For some, it would be a powerful emotional reaction or trigger. Who you are, what experiences you've lived, and in particular what your Money Design is composed of at that moment, will determine how you react emotionally and what actions you take. Even though it might be hard to believe, a person's bank account balance or annual income has little to do with why they react the way they do. Someone who makes $250,000 a year versus someone who makes $60,000 a year might have varied responses when it comes to this tax bill. But they also might have remarkably similar responses, even though they are in vastly different financial situations. Anger, fear, and loss of control might arise for both even though one (on paper) likely would have a much easier time paying the bill than the other. It all comes down to their Money Design, what an unexpected bill triggers within the body and how that experience is interpreted. In this case, loss of control might come to the forefront, and this feeling of helplessness is an opportunity to dive in and see what is unresolved within their Money Design. It could be a memory or experience as a child when their parent(s) or caregiver(s) had a financial blow or loss, leaving a messy aftermath they were unable to recover from. If this experience and the related emotions weren't processed when it occurred, then likely it's still being held in the body and will flare up when something that brings up similar emotions is experienced, alerting the body to a sense of feeling unsafe.

When it comes to emotional neutrality and being able to bring more awareness to our emotional state, our intuition and trust in our gut instinct is everything. Our intuition is our personal, internal guide. So, when we're looking at working with our emotional states to support us in deconstructing our relationship to money, our emotions are flags raised by this guide within. Our intuition will lead us—repeatedly through our emotional triggers and experiences—to look at the emotional component that is keeping us from moving forward. Awareness of the emotional components helps to feed the environment in which our dreams can grow, pointing us toward our blind spots or areas where our beliefs need to shift to realize our dream. As discussed in Chapter 6, the energetic work (accessed through our intuition) is the water that feeds the seed (our dream) to support its growth as it releases the trapped emotional component from the body. Doing this helps to release the restriction and allows energy to flow more freely in the body.

So, let's take a look at how this would play out in a real-life, day-to-day situation. Candace and her partner John are frustrated that they can't seem to get out from under their debt balances. Seemingly swimming in debt, they find themselves in a familiar emotional pattern. When one of their paychecks hits their bank account and the other has landed a brand-new client, they feel relief, a temporary high, and their connection and conversation with each other feels easy and fun. The influx of cash brings that rush of reassurance. An influx of excitement and safety as the amount of money in their bank account leaves them feeling wonderful. The emotional highs they experience give way to the inevitable (for them) emotional low that's right around the corner. Hence, the high—low, feast and famine pattern which is seen too often in our society. The sense of relief when money floods in because the money always does, was balanced with the fact that their money was right back out the door, leaving them feeling anxious and stressed until the next inflow.

When we dive into their emotional states, the feelings of anxiety and stress were triggered by viewing their lower than comfortable bank account balance and allowing their minds to take them out of to understand (or watch) which left us unable to deal with them sufficiently at that time. Those unhealed experiences remain in our body, and manifest as emotional triggers when they are poked through similar experiences in our adult lives.

Which leads us back to the importance of focusing on the root cause, going below the financial pattern to the emotional body and even further past the initial emotion or feeling. In the above story, the root of Candace's worry (i.e. the pattern of high–low) isn't really about the lack of funds, although that is a very real situation for her; the root of the worry likely stems from an incident in her childhood. It could be that her parents worried about how they would pay their bills, and she experienced that worry month after month feeling helpless and unable to do anything constructive. Because it was never resolved in her body as a child, Candace embodies these emotions as if they were her own and carries the very real financial pattern along with her into her adult relationships.

Money is simply a lens through which we can dive into the work that helps to fuel our growth, because *psst! It's not really about the money.* You could find yourself diving in through your patterns and triggers in interpersonal relationships and still find yourself coming back to the same root-level causes around worthiness and feeling deserving to receive. The programming that we have in our bodies and around us in our collective society is distorting our sense of value, leaving us disempowered when it comes to attracting the wealth and resources we desire, and keeping us from not taking fully aligned action toward our dreams, period. Money is simply a way—a big way—that we can address these root-level beliefs that are keeping us from creating the means to the end.

Working with our emotions when it comes to deconstructing our relationship to money is a vital component of moving into a healthy relationship where we aren't attempting to amass money to wield power in our own lives or outside of ourselves. Cultivating emotional awareness in our finances allows us to break down the beliefs that keep us from recognizing our innate power in creating wealth and fulfillment in our lives without money being our goal. Money is a tool that we receive as we move toward building, creating, and experiencing our goals and dreams. In Chapter 8 we'll explore how to bring emotional awareness techniques into your life when it comes to your relationship to money, and at the end of that chapter you'll be guided to reflect with powerful visualizations and prompts.

tative. Then walking over that bridge and into a life where money can be discussed as neutrally as what you'll have for supper that night. There are discussions, opinions to be had but nevertheless, you know you'll be fed and have a full belly before the night is over.

Our emotional triggers (whether related to money or not) are great teachers that show where our bodies are holding on to "trapped" emotional imprints related to beliefs and programs. Cultivating emotional awareness occurs by exploring how we can work with our emotions when it comes to deconstructing our relationship to money, tearing down the belief that money is the source of our power. Seeing that money can wield great influence allows us to recognize that it isn't the only tool that can get us to our end goals and dreams. When we focus on shifting internally first, rather than externally focusing on what we can "do" and how much money we can amass, we can shift what we're able to create. Getting to this place requires looking at our emotional states relating to money. So, if we think about how we can work with our emotions when it comes to deconstructing our relationship to money, what does that actually look like?

When we look at our day-to-day reality, working with emotions can appear like this: *bringing awareness to your emotional states and acknowledging them to create space for new beliefs to enter your life that support you in choosing a new reality.*

Your outer world is a direct reflection of your inner world, emotions included. As you bring more awareness to your Money Design, your beliefs, and your conditioning around money, emotions play a big role in how you continue to move forward in creating your financial reality. Think of emotions as the glue that binds your belief around money to your subconscious. The experiences that we are exposed to as children when it comes to money, work, finances, and our relationship with our parent(s) or caregiver(s) create neural pathways in our brains that help to reinforce particular beliefs, habits, or thoughts. The emotional states or imprints associated with these experiences are also stored within. In a sense, bonding the emotional imprint to a particular belief. It also creates a pattern in which we seek to "bond" with others and with situations as we grow up. For example, if paying bills and managing money was seen as a very stressful and chaotic occurrence to your family when you were a child, it not only imprinted those emotions to your relationship to money, but also to the beliefs that were created as you witnessed those experiences. If we can separate the emotional component from the belief, it's easier to cultivate a neutral stance with your belief and shift your perception to it. Ultimately, shifting your internal world and creating a mirrored shift externally.

Take for example, the belief "money equals power" which often translates into a belief that the person (or organization) who holds the money, has the power or influence over another individual or group of people. Let's say for an example, you grew up with a parent or caregiver who had strings attached to giving. Whether it be a gift, a loan, or helping you with something, no matter what it was, there were invisible strings attached to each energetic exchange with them, whether they realized it or not. If you were ever in a position where you needed their help and you received it, it might've left a sour taste in your mouth when it came to what was expected of you in return for what seemed like initially, a gift. In this case, there might be a stronger emotional component to receiving anything, from anyone outside of you. Resentment, regret, anger might be present in this situation as you may feel you've been cornered into something that you didn't quite have a choice about. You needed the money, gift, support, etc., so it might feel as if you've traded control over yourself in some way, shape, or form in return. When you read the statement, "money equals power," does that ring true or false in your body? Do you believe it's unequivocally true that if you have money, you have access to power over others? Even in a scenario with a sovereign individual? Check in with your body, do you feel any strong emotions related to this (on either side) or do you feel relatively neutral in your stance? And what personal experiences are swaying your opinion on the matter?

When there's an emotional charge attached to a belief around money, it can be harder to shift without accessing and processing the emotional component first. This includes beliefs around how you receive, how much you receive, or when. If there is an emotional charge in the body related to your opinion of the belief, then there is awareness that needs to be addressed first to support yourself in shifting that belief, to "unstick" the glue that is keeping that belief held as truth within your body, because *beliefs don't necessarily equal truth.* Merriam-Webster defines a belief as "something that is accepted, considered to be true, or held as an opinion."[2] To grow out of your current circumstances and expand into a new circumstance, it's necessary that you are open to questioning your current beliefs, the very things that created the experience you're in currently. Assuming and accepting our current beliefs, thoughts, and feelings as absolute truth is a surefire way to stay exactly where you are—living the same experiences on repeat. When we talk about shifting our beliefs, we're shifting internally.

2   Merriam-Webster Dictionary, "Definition of BELIEF," Merriam-webster.com, 2019, https://www.merriam-webster.com/dictionary/belief

When you can move into a state of fluidity regarding what you hold to be true, recognizing that your thoughts are more fiction than fact, you can begin to step outside yourself and bring the awareness needed to shift. Why do you believe what you believe to be true about money? About wealth? Who told you that it was true and how strongly did they believe it? When you're able to begin looking at your financial reality and what you believe to be true about money through these lenses, you can begin to poke holes into your once strongly held beliefs to make way for your next evolution and growth. As you bring more awareness into your thoughts and actions when it comes to money, you can also bring this curiosity deeper into your emotional state. As you begin examining the recurring thought or pattern, bringing more form to a belief you're holding around money, start to examine your emotional body.

Let's explore another example of a commonly held belief around money: you have to struggle to receive. I've worked with clients who held this belief, and commonly found underneath is a sense of unworthiness to receive money without working hard for it. The clients find themselves often in patterns of martyrdom: struggle, stress, and victimhood. They give all they have, tired at the end of the day, and still not receiving what they desire—only what they need. If this belief rings true for you (and it feels safe to do so), take a moment and try this exercise for yourself:

Close your eyes and take three deep breaths in and out slowly, allowing your body to relax and unwind with each breath out.

Allow yourself to sink into the chair or the bed where you're sitting, bringing attention to your body and releasing all tension to fully surrender.

In a moment you will read the statement below, and when you do, pay attention to how your body reacts—physically and emotionally.

"To receive the money I desire, I have to work hard for it."

Pay attention to:

1. Does your body react to the truth of this or does it not believe this to be true? I.e. What immediate thoughts or judgments appear? Intuitively do you resonate for or against this statement?
2. How does your physical and emotional body react to this statement? Do you feel any area of your body tighten? Restrict? Does any emotion rise to your chest or sink into your belly?

Take a moment to explore what your body has to tell you right now.

This is one way to bring awareness to your emotional state. Identify a belief first through awareness in your day-to-day interactions, then allow your body to show you how it feels emotionally. More commonly, this process is reversed. We bring awareness to the heightened emotional state (or trigger) during an experience, then work backward to identify the belief that is tied to this emotional reaction. Let's look at how this might crop up in your life using the same belief as the example: In order to receive the money I desire, I have to work hard for it.

You're at the office at the end of a really long day. You watch as your employees walk out the door at 5:00 p.m., 5:01 p.m., 5:05 p.m. and your anger and frustration start to build as you tell yourself that you're going to be here for hours finishing up the work that needs to be done. Why does everything fall on your shoulders? Wasn't owning a business supposed to feel easier than this? Where's the freedom you were promised? You walk back to the kitchen to grab another cup of coffee to fuel yourself as you prepare for the long night ahead.

In this example the emotional reaction of anger and frustration building in the chest is the first indicator that the body is trying to tell you something. You can say, of course, "why wouldn't I be mad? Everyone's leaving and I'm left with all of this on my plate!" But let's step back and assume that the emotional trigger has a message, and we should follow your body's lead and explore. If I was working with this client, I would recommend she bring awareness and curiosity into the experience as soon as she realized that she felt ungrounded and "off." Then, if it feels emotionally safe to do so, she'd follow these steps after taking a few deep breaths and grounding herself:

1. Name the emotions she was experiencing within her body: anger, frustration, resentment.
2. Identify where she is physically experiencing these emotions in the body, such as rising from the abdomen and into the chest. Then take it a step further by exploring the size, texture, or shape of the emotion. Does it feel heavy or light? Hard or soft? Shaped like a rock or slim like a feather? Bring as much detail as she can to this awareness stage inside her body.
3. Allow space to process the emotion and discover what's behind it. She might ask herself why she's angry and frustrated (assuming the emotional trigger is not heightened to a state that wouldn't allow critical thinking). Take time to sit in reflection or journal on the reasons why she's experiencing these emotions. It might begin as

a.k.a. a flight response, while the parasympathetic nervous system provides the "brakes." Dianne suggests that the brakes look like "lowering the heart rate and relaxing the muscles so that the body can return to passive behavior."[3] Our nervous systems have evolved from these two primitive states to include a third state called a "ventral vagal complex" which contributes to our ability to feel safe and secure in our modern society, rather than assuming everything that we come into contact with is a threat.[4] In the previous example, when the anger or frustration was triggered, it created a sympathetic nervous system response in the body. This makes it hard to reason, see the reality of the situation, or even pay attention closely to what our body is trying to tell us, as the experience contradicts the reality (in this example, her goals) that we want to experience.

When in a sympathetic nervous state, it can be difficult to examine your emotional state without spiraling into a more extreme state of heightened emotions, which might leave you feeling worse than when you started and make it harder to shake the "bad mood." That's why it's recommended to bring a sense of calm and grounding to your nervous system before you begin to identify and break down the emotion into its root belief. And if you are not able to do so on your own, seek professional help to support you in unraveling here. A great self-healing technique called grounding can help you move into a parasympathetic state where it is easier to disrupt the pattern (in this example the pattern of feeling angry and frustrated when left feeling unsupported) and identify and begin to work with the root belief.

3   Dianne Grande, "The Neuroscience of Feeling Safe and Connected," *Psychology Today*, September 24, 2018, https://www.psychologytoday.com/us/blog/in-it-together/201809/the-neuroscience-feeling-safe-and-connected

4   Grande, "The Neuroscience"

According to *Healthline*, grounding can also be referred to as earthing and "is a therapeutic technique that involves activities that ground or electrically reconnect you to the earth."[5] According to this article, the practice includes physical connection to nature (i.e. walking barefoot on the grass), using grounding mats, or other tools to help you experience this effect while indoors. While these are incredible tools that can bring you into this state of being, I've also found that visualization (which doesn't have the scientific backing to help us understand why this works) also does the trick—and oftentimes it is much faster. Have you ever listened to a guided meditation? Done a yoga class? Listened to a soothing audio track to help you sleep? Listening to these audio tracks or being guided in this way can quickly bring you back into the present moment, to your body, and bring calm almost instantly. This process is what I refer to when I recommend grounding your body. Using visualization or meditation to reconnect your awareness to your body (which is from the Earth and returns to the Earth) and visually connecting into the ground to support your balance and recalibrate your energy. Bringing you into a place where you feel safe and supported to dive deeper into the emotional states that are present in the emotional trigger.

Once you're able to reach a grounded state in your body, it can feel much easier to go back through the steps outlined above, starting with naming the emotion and moving through to bringing hyperawareness to your thoughts and beliefs. At the end of this chapter, within the reflection for Section 2, I've included an audio recording that will take you through a grounding visualization to support you as you begin to explore

---

5   Eleesha Lockett, "What Is Grounding and Can It Help Improve Your Health?," *Healthline*, August 30, 2019, https://www.healthline.com/health/grounding

and cultivate these practices for your growth toward your dreams. Bringing awareness to your patterns and emotional states while bringing in a grounding practice can help you to begin processing the emotional states that are keeping you from neutrality in your relationship to money.

In the next section we'll dive deeper into what comes next after cultivating this awareness from a grounded state and how you can begin to heal at the root to release yourself from the beliefs that are no longer supporting you in reaching your desired financial reality.

REFLECTION 2: PAUSE - REFLECT - PROCESS

To access the e-course that accompanies this book, enter www.moremoneymorepowerbook.com in your web browser. After entering your e-mail address you will have access to the visualizations and reflection workbooks that were designed to help you deepen the work within these pages. Below are the reflection questions and activities that you can take to deepen the work from Section 2: Chapters 6 through 8. If you'd rather print a workbook to use, you can access it with the above link along with your guided visualizations.

Below are the accompanying reflection questions to help you deepen the work while listening to the recordings or for further support afterward, for Chapter 6 through 8:

1. In Chapter 6 we talked about visualizing your "dream life." When you did this, in what ways did your dream life visualization differ from what your parent(s), caregiver(s), and/or sibling(s) would desire for their life? And what would they, or do they, say about your life now and what you desire?

   _____

   _____

   _____

   _____

   _____

   _____

   _____

   _____

5. After reading through Section 2, what habitual emotional triggers can you recall experiencing in your life surrounding your finances? What are the primary emotions that rise to the surface when you think about your current financial situation? If you think about the common triggers that arise around your finances, how do those make you feel?

   Write out an exhaustive list, if it feels safe to do so, then take yourself through question 6 and 7 using the most common trigger and emotion.

   _____

   _____

   _____

   _____

   _____

   _____

   _____

   _____

   _____

   _____

   _____

   _____

   _____

   _____

6. After listening to the grounding visualization, answer the below questions. How did you feel before and after the grounding visualization? How did you notice your physical body shift in response to the exercise?

_____

_____

_____

_____

_____

_____

_____

7. Bringing awareness to your patterns and emotional states while bringing in a grounding practice can help you to begin processing the emotional states that are keeping you from neutrality in your relationship to money. Reflect below on how you can begin to create a practice where you can explore your emotional experiences safely when it comes to your financial triggers.

_____

_____

_____

_____

_____

_____

_____

RECLAIM

ity through your beliefs. Continued shifts in awareness will lead to new choices, and new choices make way for new realities. In a sense, your brain and body are retrained to believe a different reality with money. As you reprogram your body in this way, your internal world shifts which triggers a shift in your external world concurrently. Because we are what we believe.

This process can be used repeatedly as you move through your day-to-day life to help bring awareness to how your current Money Design might not support your growth in reaching your goals. Since you're here, reading this book, I'm going to guess you care about growth. You have dreams and a vision that you are working toward, and therefore, want more than what you currently are experiencing in this life. Acquiring money and other resources is likely a large part of that creation experience for you, a necessary tool as you continue on this journey. So, the more you become aware of the ways you are conditioned to receive and expend money, the easier it is to shift into a belief that allows you to experience what you desire while more easily receiving money. To create wealth, activate your innate power, and bring the influence you desire to this world; your focus must remain on your fulfillment, not on money or grasping for power. Awareness is the key to begin disrupting patterns while identifying and shifting beliefs. The decision point is the next step to disrupt patterns. Why do you see, and know, and feel your habitual, detrimental patterns around money, but still continue to find yourself in them? Because they are quite literally ingrained in your body. The para-sympathetic and sympathetic nervous states, and the neural pathways in your brain that hold the emotional imprint along with the belief, all play a role in shifting you in or out of a pattern. Let's take an example to showcase this. Emmanuel is a self-employed marketing consultant. He pays himself a salary and doesn't withhold taxes, nor does he pay quarterly taxes (let's ignore the fact that he might be required to pay quarterly taxes depending on his individual circumstances and keep this simple). He knows that come tax time he will be required to come up with a rather large sum of money to pay his taxes, so each month he will set aside cash toward his tax bill. Typically in the fall, he experiences a low period in his business as people get ready for the holidays, and he finds himself unable to meet his monthly needs and living expenses. Each year he dips into his tax bill fund and promises himself that he'll replenish it as he heads into the new year, leaving it for "future Emmanuel" to take care of.

After the new year rolls around, he finds himself scrambling as he receives notice from his accountant that his tax bill is $8,000 more than what he has in his account. Anxiety, fear, and panic set in. Over the next few months he finds himself moving in and out of those emotions while he scrambles; selling discounted services to ramp up business, cutting back on all outings with his friends, eating in for every meal and skimping on his typical lifestyle. By tax time he somehow pulls together the extra $8,000 and is able to pay his tax bill at the deadline. Relief floods him. Then panic ensues again as he quickly realizes that he has to start rebuilding the account as there's nothing left, and it's already a third of the way through the year! That panic fades as he again deems it "future Emmanuel's" problem to take care of, and he allows himself to set money aside *as he can* until the holidays roll around, just in time to do it all over again. This is Emmanuel's pattern that he has experienced every year since he became a business owner. The emotional highs and lows throughout the year also mirror him moving in and out of the sympathetic state (the state that turns struggle and hardship; or that he dislikes paying taxes to the government on his self-employed income and is unknowingly keeping that balance low as he harbors resentment. As the root of these beliefs begin to surface, he can use energetic techniques to support his body, ultimately release the emotional component, and shift the belief into something supportive. As this shift occurs, he will likely feel more stable, safe, and secure as he makes decisions for the future. This allows him to take perceived risks toward creating his personal and professional life in a way that lights him up and fulfills him without making decisions purely to avoid pain. allowing himself to move forward led by love, for himself. Stripping away the conditioning given to us allows us to let our own bright lights shine, knowing that we are living more fully in our purpose.

Through this example and others throughout the book, you can see how deeply personal this process can be. We are uniquely designed—not only physically, but our energetic imprint as well. When we're looking at Money Design, fraternal twins raised by the same parents could walk away from their childhood with varying degrees of comfort regarding how much and in what way they receive in their lives. This could be based on firsthand experiences, witnessed experiences, environmental differences, and a multitude of other factors. This work isn't for the faint of heart, it requires us to be open and willing to look at the dark corners of our lives, our childhood, and where our other patterns were created.

The number one thing this work is? It's empowering. It empowers you to step into the role of self-healer as you reclaim your power, because we all are our own greatest healers. Picking up tools, techniques, and pieces of awareness along the way as you deconstruct your relationship to money, power, and inner fulfillment. Because it's not really about money. Money has been put up on a pedestal and as such, is keeping us separated from our innate power. Separate, disillusioned, and unfulfilled. Keeping us on a never-ending quest for more, to fill the space within that can never be filled by anything outside of us. When I think of how our souls came into this world, I believe we came in whole. Complete. And many of us are here at this moment on Earth to help in our own way both personally and collectively, to shift our societal structures, money included. And allowing money to return to a neutral tool, one that no longer needs to keep us separate from our truth. The truth that power isn't derived from amassing money, because that power is already inside of you, ready to be seen. It's not something that's given to you or earned. It's waiting for you to reclaim. The biggest fallacy that is helping to keep our society from further evolving into a state where we are working within societal structures that are built on love, is believing that we need *more* to wield our power, when it's already inside of us.

There is so much power in the healing done on an individual level as you look at the collective experience. Imagine if each person who undertakes the work of deconstructing their relationship to money, moving it into a neutral tool, and stripping the power we've given to it, begins to emit a bright light that turns on as they access and step into their personal power. If each person who lets go of beliefs, restructures their inner world to align with the soul-led purpose they're here to experience, allows their light to shine. One by one these bright lights converge into bigger lights, helping to energetically shift the very structures that are used to support our interactions with money. There is power in awareness, intention, and engagement.

supported at a base level each second of every day that we are on this Earth. Why would allowing money—also an energy form—to support you be any different from allowing the air and the sun to support you as you go in and out of each day? Why are you worthy to receive one more than the other?

The truth is, it shouldn't be any different.

It's the societal conditioning, programming, and beliefs that keep us from believing that we can have whatever it is we need. It keeps you from knowing that what you desire to create, to experience, also desires you. There's just likely some shifting of perception within your Money Design to allow yourself to receive at a greater level, and that's why our paths have crossed. Deconstructing your programming around money will help to remove and release the programs and beliefs that make you believe anything but the fact that you can have, be, do whatever it is you desire. You are worthy of receiving it all because your desires are yours. They were given to you, not as a cruel joke for you to pine over and never have the pleasure of experiencing; they're yours to cultivate, to grow, and to enjoy. If you think of your goals, your desires, your vision as having an energy or entity of their own, you can imagine how they decided to partner with you. Why else would they be hanging around, whispering in your ear, popping in and out of your dreams as you plan for the future? That's why I encourage you to stack the deck in your favor. Give yourself the gift of cultivating the tools needed to deconstruct your programming around money that doesn't support you as you align with your dreams.

Pieces of your Money Design are apparent when you start to bring awareness into the equation by getting into the "now" moment. In the "now" moment you're aware of your current experience: what's happening around you in your environment, how you feel, and what your present thoughts are. As we covered previously, you can't believe everything you think, simply because your thoughts are not the truth. The more we can bring presence and attention to your current thoughts, the easier it is to separate yourself from them and no longer claim them as your own, especially when your current thoughts are a big part of creating your current reality. If you desire change, it's important to bring attention to those habitual thoughts that aren't supportive of your goals, dreams, and desires. You can allow them to simply be what they are: subconscious, conditioned thoughts, ideas, opinions that are happening in response to what's occurring in front of you at any given moment. The more you can interrupt the conditioned flow of your thoughts, redirect them, and question them, the easier it will be to cultivate awareness to shift them. Not because how you are right now is wrong or bad, but because what your conditioned thought train is doing right this very second might not be supporting you in creating the reality you desire to move into. No judgment, no shame, just curiosity toward what your body is presenting at any given moment. If you are seeing the same patterns in your life on repeat, I'm going to guess that you're also thinking the same thoughts and experiencing the same conditioned responses on repeat. Your current thoughts are helping to create the reality before you now. If you want to change, pay attention to your body: the audio track running through your mind, your emotional state and how you react to the world around you, and your intuition. Because anything can happen at any moment, truly. Your future can shift in any direction when you get into the present and wield your power as a conscious creator.

ble change with intentionality? Direct it towards what it is you desire, rather than allowing your subconscious patterns and habits to call the shots as you move forward towards your goals? The opportunities are untold when you move with intentionality and do the inner work to allow your actions to support your intentions. I applaud you for taking an important step (whether this book and e-course was your first or one hundredth) when it comes to shifting your perception and relationship to money. My hope for you is that these teachings have opened up new doorways that weren't visible to you prior to picking up this book; that greater possibilities are floating into your awareness; and you are opening up to the trust that the support you need to walk through those doors will arrive in divine time.

To move into this new embodied state—of love and possibility—it requires an honest look at your relationship to money. And within this relationship, ensure you hold the belief that you are worthy and deserve to receive what it is you desire. Come back to the truth that you are worthy to receive simply for existing; this is your destination. Take money off its pedestal, reclaim your power, and walk boldly towards what it is you desire—know that it's yours to claim. Now it's time to take this newfound awareness and possibility into action, turn the page where you will be prompted to access the last section of your e-course.

I am so grateful that you chose to join me and tap into the energy and teachings within this book and accompanying e-course. I hope these words have activated new awareness and possibility that will guide you to begin uncovering your Money Design and shift it to further align with your vision and dreams. If you have not already intentionally paused within the book to access your e-course, I recommend you do so now after completing the book. The book and e-course go hand in hand, designed to take you deeper and begin implementing and taking action on the teachings within *More Money, More Power?*.

This book was created and intended to meet you where are, right now. My hope is that if you feel called to pick up this book a year or even ten years from now that you will have a wildly different experience. The e-course is a guided journey that can only take you as far as you are willing, and if you're open and ready for change your body will adjust accordingly as you allow it to lead. Take the tools within both the book and e-course to support you as you continue to shift in your day-to-day life. Take the inspiration, ideas, and awareness you've cultivated throughout and put them into action. Create space to intentionally create your goals, then allow your habits to shift to support you in experiencing those goals. Awareness precedes choice, but nothing will change if you don't put it into practice. Use the e-course, a friend, or this newfound community to support you as you hold yourself accountable to the change you desire to see.

As this love letter (in the form of a book and e-course) from the Universe to your soul signs off, I hope you take this awareness with you as you create and experience your wildest dreams within your incredible corner of the world. That you take this permission slip to boldly step onto your throne knowing you are whole and worthy now to receive all that you desire. And that you accept the possibility that the fulfillment you long for is within your reach, and all it takes is a look within.

Darcie Elizabeth

www.moremoneymorepowerbook.com

Darcie Elizabeth is an energetic business consultant, international best-selling author, speaker, and CPA (inactive) committed to changing the way the world moves forward with money. She guides and teaches business owners, visionaries, and way-showers to discover their key to attracting more and manifesting with ease through deconstructing their relationship to money. Diving in with the lens of your unique Money Design, a term used to encompass the subconscious reality dictating why you do what you do with money, you can attract the resources needed to see your goals and vision through to reality. With over a decade of experience in the financial industry and as a trained energy practitioner, she's equipped to support holistically, the above and below the surface aspects of money. Darcie works with clients on a one-on-one basis and within group settings, virtually. She also inspires and educates groups as a speaker and workshop facilitator all to support her mission: to help shift the way the world interacts and engages with money into an empowered state for all.

GOLDEN BRICK ROAD
PUBLISHING HOUSE

Link arms with us as we pave new paths to a better and more expansive world.

Golden Brick Road Publishing House (GBRPH) is a small, independently initiated boutique press created to provide social-innovation entrepreneurs, experts, and leaders a space in which they can develop their writing skills and content to reach existing audiences as well as new readers.

Serving an ambitious catalogue of books by individual authors, GBRPH also boasts a unique co-author program that capitalizes on the concept of "many hands make light work." GBRPH works with our authors as partners. Thanks to the value, originality, and fresh ideas we provide our readers, GBRPH books have won ten awards and are now available in bookstores across North America.

We aim to develop content that effects positive social change while empowering and educating our members to help them strengthen themselves and the services they provide to their clients.

Iconoclastic, ambitious, and set to enable social innovation, GBRPH is helping our writers/partners make cultural change one book at a time.

Inquire today at www.goldenbrickroad.pub